Decision Making Using Game Theory

An Introduction for Managers

Game theory is a key element in most decision-making processes involving two or more people or organisations. This book explains how game theory can predict the outcome of complex decision-making processes, and how it can help you to improve your own negotiation and decision-making skills. It is grounded in well-established theory, yet the wide-ranging international examples used to illustrate its application offer a fresh approach to what is becoming an essential weapon in the armoury of the informed manager. The book is accessibly written, explaining in simple terms the underlying mathematics behind games of skill, before moving on to more sophisticated topics such as zero-sum games, mixed-motive games, and multi-person games, coalitions and power. Clear examples and helpful diagrams are used throughout, and the mathematics is kept to a minimum. It is written for managers, students and decision makers in any field.

Dr Anthony Kelly is a lecturer at the University of Southampton Research & Graduate School of Education where he teaches game theory and decision making to managers and students.

Decision Making using Game Theory

An introduction for managers

Anthony Kelly

CAMBRIDGE
UNIVERSITY PRESS

PUBLISHED BY THE PRESS SYNDICATE OF THE UNIVERSITY OF CAMBRIDGE
The Pitt Building, Trumpington Street, Cambridge, United Kingdom

CAMBRIDGE UNIVERSITY PRESS
The Edinburgh Building, Cambridge CB2 2RU, UK
40 West 20th Street, New York, NY 10011-4211, USA
477 Williamstown Road, Port Melbourne, VIC 3207, Australia
Ruiz de Alarcón 13, 28014 Madrid, Spain
Dock House, The Waterfront, Cape Town 8001, South Africa

http://www.cambridge.org

First published 2003

Printed in the United Kingdom at the University Press, Cambridge

Typeface Minion 11.5/14pt   *System* Poltype® [v n]

A catalogue record for this book is available from the British Library

Library of Congress Cataloguing in Publication data

Kelly, Anthony, 1957–
Decision making using game theory: An introduction for managers / Anthony Kelly
    p.   cm.
Includes bibliographical references and index.
ISBN 0 521 81462 6
1. Game theory   I. Title.

HB144 .K45 2002
658.4'0353–dc21   2002019217

ISBN 0 521 81462 6 hardback

Contents

Preface

And, greatest dread of all, the dread of games!

John Betjeman 1906–1984 'Summoned by Bells'

Game theory is the science of strategic decision making. It is a powerful tool in understanding the relationships that are made and broken in the course of competition and cooperation. It is not a panacea for the shortcomings of bad management. For managers, or those who interact with management, it is simply an alternative perspective with which to view the process of problem solving. It is a tool, which, like all others, is best used by those who reflect on their own practice as a mechanism for improvement. Chance favours a prepared mind and this book is intended as much for those who are seeking effectiveness as for those who have already found it.

Game theory has been used to great effect in sciences as diverse as evolutionary biology and economics, so books on the subject abound. They vary from the esoteric to the populist; from the pedantic to the frivolous. This book is different in a number of ways. It is designed for both students and practitioners. It is theoretical insofar as it provides an introduction to the science and mathematics of game theory; and practical in that it offers a praxis of that theory to illustrate the resolution of problems common to management in both the commercial and the not-for-profit sectors.

The book is intended to help managers in a number of ways:
- To expand the conceptual framework within which managers operate and in doing so, encourage them to develop more powerful generic problem-solving skills.
- To resolve practical difficulties as and when they occur, more efficiently and with increased effectiveness.

- To find new solutions to familiar problems that have not been satisfactorily resolved, by giving practitioners a deeper understanding of the nature of incentives, conflict, bargaining, decision making and cooperation.
- To offer an alternative perspective on problems, both old and new, which may or may not yield solutions, but which at worst, will lead to an increased understanding of the objective nature of strategic decision making.
- To help managers understand the nature of power in multi-person systems and thereby reduce the perception of disenfranchisement among those who work in committee-like structures within organisations.

The book is a self-contained, though by no means exhaustive, study of game theory. It is primarily intended for those who work as managers, but not exclusively so. Students of politics, economics, management science, psychology and education may find the approach used here more accessible than the usual format of books on the subject. No great mathematical prowess is required beyond a familiarity with elementary calculus and algebra in two variables.

Game theory, by its very nature, offers a rational perspective and, in a society that has developed an aversion to such things, this will be sufficient reason for some to criticise it. This is as unfortunate as it is short-sighted. Research suggests that good managers are well informed, multi-skilled and flexible in their approach to problem solving. Organisations themselves are increasingly complex places, which can no longer afford to live in isolation from the expectations of their employees or the wider community. More than ever, they are workplaces where managers must continuously balance opposing forces. The resulting tensions are ever-changing, and know-how, mathematical or otherwise, is often what separates a failing manager from a successful one.

It has been said, by way of an excuse for curtailing knowledge, that a person with two watches never knows what time it is! Unfortunately, managers cannot afford such blinkered luxury. Game theory has clearly been successful in describing, at least in part, what it is to be a decision maker today and this book is for those who are willing to risk knowing more.

1 Introduction

Man is a gaming animal. He must always be trying to get the better in something or other.

Charles Lamb 1775–1834 'Essays of Elia'

Game theory is the theory of independent and interdependent decision making. It is concerned with decision making in organisations where the outcome depends on the decisions of two or more autonomous players, one of which may be nature itself, and where no single decision maker has full control over the outcomes. Obviously, games like chess and bridge fall within the ambit of game theory, but so do many other social situations which are not commonly regarded as games in the everyday sense of the word.

Classical models fail to deal with interdependent decision making because they treat players as inanimate subjects. They are cause and effect models that neglect the fact that people make decisions that are consciously influenced by what others decide. A game theory model, on the other hand, is constructed around the strategic choices available to players, where the preferred outcomes are clearly defined and known.

Consider the following situation. Two cyclists are going in opposite directions along a narrow path. They are due to collide and it is in both their interests to avoid such a collision. Each has three strategies: move to the right; move to the left; or maintain direction. Obviously, the outcome depends on the decisions of both cyclists and their interests coincide exactly. This is a fully *cooperative game* and the players need to signal their intentions to one other.

However, sometimes the interests of players can be completely opposed. Say, for example, that a number of retail outlets are each

1

vying for business from a common finite catchment area. Each has to decide whether or not to reduce prices, without knowing what the others have decided. Assuming that turnover increases when prices are dropped, various strategic combinations result in gains or losses for some of the retailers, but if one retailer gains customers, another must lose them. So this is a *zero-sum non-cooperative game* and unlike cooperative games, players need to conceal their intentions from each other.

A third category of game represents situations where the interests of players are partly opposed and partly coincident. Say, for example, the teachers' union at a school is threatening not to participate in parents' evenings unless management rescinds the redundancy notice of a long-serving colleague. Management refuses. The union now complicates the game by additionally threatening not to cooperate with preparations for government inspection, if their demands are not met. Management has a choice between conceding and refusing, and whichever option it selects, the union has four choices: to resume both normal work practices; to participate in parents' evenings only; to participate in preparations for the inspection only; or not to resume participation in either. Only one of the possible strategic combinations leads to a satisfactory outcome from the management's point of view – management refusing to meet the union's demands notwithstanding the resumption of normal work – although clearly some outcomes are worse than others. Both players (management and union) prefer some outcomes to others. For example, both would rather see a resumption of participation in parents' evenings – since staff live in the community and enrolment depends on it – than not to resume participation in either. So the players' interests are simultaneously opposed and coincident. This is an example of a *mixed-motive game.*

Game theory aims to find optimal solutions to situations of conflict and cooperation such as those outlined above, under the assumption that players are instrumentally rational and act in their own best interests. In some cases, solutions can be found. In others, although formal attempts at a solution may fail, the analytical synthesis itself can illuminate different facets of the problem. Either way, game theory offers an interesting perspective on the nature of strategic selection in both familiar and unusual circumstances.

The assumption of rationality can be justified on a number of levels.

At its most basic level, it can be argued that players behave rationally by instinct, although experience suggests that this is not always the case, since decision makers frequently adopt simplistic algorithms which lead to sub-optimal solutions.

Secondly, it can be argued that there is a kind of 'natural selection' at work which inclines a group of decisions towards the rational and optimal. In business, for example, organisations that select sub-optimal strategies eventually shut down in the face of competition from optimising organisations. Thus, successive generations of decisions are increasingly rational, though the extent to which this competitive evolution transfers to not-for-profit sectors like education and the public services, is unclear.

Finally, it has been suggested that the assumption of rationality that underpins game theory is not an attempt to describe how players actually make decisions, but merely that they behave *as if* they were not irrational (Friedman, 1953). All theories and models are, by definition, simplifications and should not be dismissed simply because they fail to represent all realistic possibilities. A model should only be discarded if its predictions are false or useless, and game theoretic models are neither. Indeed, as with scientific theories, minor departures from full realism can often lead to a greater understanding of the issues (Romp, 1997).

Terminology

Game theory represents an abstract model of decision making, not the social reality of decision making itself. Therefore, while game theory ensures that a result follows logically from a model, it cannot ensure that the result itself represents reality, except in so far as the model is an accurate one. To describe this model accurately requires practitioners to share a common language which, to the uninitiated, might seem excessively technical. This is unavoidable. Since game theory represents the interface of mathematics and management, it must of necessity adopt a terminology that is familiar to both.

The basic constituents of any game are its participating, autonomous decision makers, called *players*. Players may be individual persons, organisations or, in some cases, nature itself. When nature is designated as one of the players, it is assumed that it moves without favour and according to the laws of chance. In the terminology of game theory, nature is not 'counted' as one of the players. So, for example, when a deck of cards is shuffled prior to a game of solitaire, nature – the second player – is making the first move in what is a 'one-player' game. This is intrinsically different from chess for example, where nature takes no part initially or subsequently.

A game must have two or more players, one of which may be nature. The total number of players may be large, but must be finite and must be known. Each player must have more than one choice, because a player with only one way of selecting can have no strategy and therefore cannot alter the outcome of a game.

An *outcome* is the result of a complete set of strategic selections by all the players in a game and it is assumed that players have consistent preferences among the possibilities. Furthermore, it is assumed that individuals are capable of arranging these possible outcomes in some order of preference. If a player is indifferent to the difference between two or more outcomes, then those outcomes are assigned equal rank. Based on this order of preference, it is possible to assign numeric pay-offs to all possible outcomes. In some games, an ordinal scale is sufficient, but in others, it is necessary to have interval scales where preferences are set out in proportional terms. For example, a pay-off of six should be three times more desirable than a pay-off of two.

A *pure strategy* for a player is a campaign plan for the entire game, stipulating in advance what the player will do in response to every eventuality. If a player selects a strategy without knowing which strategies were chosen by the other players, then the player's pure strategies are simply equivalent to his or her choices. If, on the other hand, a player's strategy is selected subsequent to those of other players and knowing what they were, then there will be more pure strategies than choices. For example, in the case of the union dispute cited above, management has two choices and two pure strategies: concede or refuse. However, the union's strategic selection is made after management's strategic selection and in full knowledge of it, so their pure strategies are advance statements of what the union will select in response to each of management's selections. Consequently, although the union has only four choices (to resume both practices; to participate in parents' evenings only; to participate in preparations for gov-

Table 1.1 The union's pure strategies

If management chooses to . . .	Then the union will . . .	And if management chooses to . . .	Then the union will . . .
Concede	Resume both practices	Refuse	Resume both practices
Concede	Resume both practices	Refuse	Resume parents' evenings
Concede	Resume both practices	Refuse	Resume inspection preparations
Concede	Resume both practices	Refuse	Resume neither practice
Concede	Resume parents' evenings	Refuse	Resume both practices
Concede	Resume parents' evenings	Refuse	Resume parents' evenings
Concede	Resume parents' evenings	Refuse	Resume inspection preparations
Concede	Resume parents' evenings	Refuse	Resume neither practice
Concede	Resume Ofsted preparations	Refuse	Resume both practices
Concede	Resume Ofsted preparations	Refuse	Resume parents' evenings
Concede	Resume Ofsted preparations	Refuse	Resume inspection preparations
Concede	Resume Ofsted preparations	Refuse	Resume neither practice
Concede	Resume neither practice	Refuse	Resume both practices
Concede	Resume neither practice	Refuse	Resume parents' evenings
Concede	Resume neither practice	Refuse	Resume inspection preparations
Concede	Resume neither practice	Refuse	Resume neither practice

ernment inspection only; not to resume participation in either), they have 16 pure strategies, as set out in Table 1.1 above. Some of them may appear nonsensical, but that does not preclude them from consideration, as many managers have found to their cost!

In a game of *complete information*, players know their own strategies and pay-off functions and those of other players. In addition, each player knows that the other players have complete information. In games of *incomplete information*, players know the rules of the game and their own preferences of course, but not the pay-off functions of the other players.

A game of *perfect information* is one in which players select strategies sequentially and are aware of what other players have already chosen, like chess. A game of *imperfect information* is one in which players have to act in ignorance of one another's moves, merely anticipating what the other player will do.

Classifying games

There are three categories of games: games of *skill*; games of *chance*; and games of *strategy*. Games of skill are one-player games whose defining property is the existence of a single player who has complete control over all the outcomes. Sitting an examination is one example. Games of skill should not really be classified as games at all, since the ingredient of interdependence is missing. Nevertheless, they are discussed in the next chapter because they have many applications in management situations.

Games of chance are one-player games against nature. Unlike games of skill, the player does not control the outcomes completely and strategic selections do not lead inexorably to certain outcomes. The outcomes of a game of chance depend partly on the player's choices and partly on nature, who is a second player. Games of chance are further categorised as either involving risk or involving uncertainty. In the former, the player knows the probability of each of nature's responses and therefore knows the probability of success for each of his or her strategies. In games of chance involving uncertainty, probabilities cannot meaningfully be assigned to any of nature's responses (Colman, 1982), so the player's outcomes are uncertain and the probability of success unknown.

Games of strategy are games involving two or more players, not including nature, each of whom has partial control over the outcomes. In a way, since the players cannot assign probabilities to each other's choices, games of strategy are games involving uncertainty. They can be sub-divided into two-player games and multi-player games. Within each of these two sub-divisions, there are three further sub-categories depending on the way in which the pay-off functions are related to one another – whether the player's interests are completely coincident; completely conflicting; or partly coincident and party conflicting:

- Games of strategy, whether two-player or multi-player, in which the players' interests coincide, are called *cooperative games of strategy*.
- Games in which the players' interests are conflicting (i.e. strictly competitive games) are known as *zero-sum games of strategy*, so called because the pay-offs always add up to zero for each outcome of a fair game, or to another constant if the game is biased.

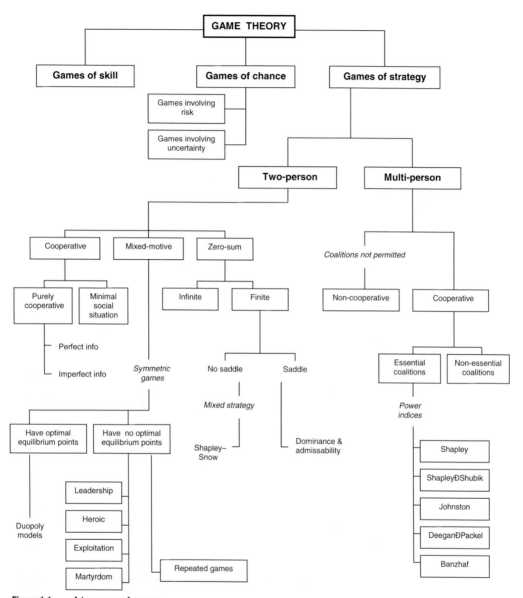

Figure 1.1   A taxonomy of games.

- Games in which the interests of players are neither fully conflicting nor fully coincident are called *mixed-motive games of strategy*.

Of the three categories, this last one represents most realistically the intricacies of social interaction and interdependent decision making and most game theory is concentrated on it.

A brief history of game theory

Game theory was conceived in the seventeenth century by mathematicians attempting to solve the gambling problems of the idle French nobility, evidenced for example by the correspondence of Pascal and Fermat (*c.* 1650) concerning the amusement of an aristocrat called de Mere (Colman, 1982; David, 1962). In these early days, largely as a result of its origins in parlour games such as chess, game theory was preoccupied with two-person zero-sum interactions. This rendered it less than useful as an application to fields like economics and politics, and the earliest record of such use is the 1881 work of Francis Edgeworth, rediscovered in 1959 by Martin Shubik.

Game theory in the modern era was ushered in with the publication in 1913, by the German mathematician Ernst Zermelo, of *Uber eine Anwendung der Mengenlehre auf die Theorie des Schachspiels*, in which he proved that every competitive two-person game possesses a best strategy for both players, provided both players have complete information about each other's intentions and preferences. Zermelo's theorem was quickly followed by others, most notably by the minimax theorem, which states that there exists a strategy for each player in a competitive game, such that none of the players regret their choice of strategy when the game is over. The minimax theorem became the fundamental theorem of game theory, although its genesis predated Zermelo by two centuries. In 1713, an Englishman, James Waldegrave (whose mother was the daughter of James II) proposed a minimax-type solution to a popular two-person card game of the period, though he made no attempt to generalise his findings (Dimand & Dimand, 1992). The discovery did not attract any great attention, save for a mention in correspondence between Pierre de Montmort and Nicholas Bernouilli. It appears not to have unduly distracted Waldegrave either, for by 1721, he had become a career diplomat, serving as British ambassador to the Hapsburg court in Vienna. Nevertheless, by 1865, Waldegrave's solution was deemed significant enough to be included in Isaac Todhunter's *A History of the Mathematical Theory of Probability*, an authoritative, if somewhat dreary, tome. Waldegrave's contribution might have attracted more attention but for that dreariness and his minimax-type solution remained largely unknown at the start of the twentieth century.

In 1921, the eminent French academician Emile Borel began publishing on gaming strategies, building on the work of Zermelo and others. Over the course of the next six years, he published five papers on the subject, including the first modern formulation of a mixed-strategy game. He appears to have been unaware of Waldegrave's earlier work. Borel (1924) attempted, but failed, to prove the minimax theorem. He went so far as to suggest that it could never be proved, but as is so often the case with rash predictions, he was promptly proved wrong! The minimax theorem was proved for the general case in December 1926, by the Hungarian mathematician, John von Neumann. The complicated proof, published in 1928, was subsequently modified by von Neumann himself (1937), Jean Ville (1938), Hermann Weyl (1950) and others. Its predictions were later verified by experiment to be accurate to within one per cent and it remains a keystone in game theoretic constructions (O'Neill, 1987).

Borel claimed priority over von Neumann for the discovery of game theory. His claim was rejected, but not without some disagreement. Even as late as 1953, Maurice Frechet and von Neumann were engaged in a dispute on the relative importance of Borel's early contributions to the new science. Frechet maintained that due credit had not been paid to his colleague, while von Neumann maintained, somewhat testily, that until his minimax proof, what little had been done was of little significance anyway.

The verdict of history is probably that they did not give each other much credit. Von Neumann, tongue firmly in cheek, wrote that he considered it an honour 'to have labored on ground over which Borel had passed' (Frechet, 1953), but the natural competition that can sometimes exist between intellectuals of this stature, allied to some local Franco–German rivalry, seems to have got the better of common sense.

In addition to his prodigious academic achievements, Borel had a long and prominent career outside mathematics, winning the Croix de Guerre in the First World War, the Resistance Medal in the Second World War and serving his country as a member of parliament, Minister for the Navy and president of the prestigious Institut de France. He died in 1956.

Von Neumann found greatness too, but by a different route. He was thirty years younger than Borel, born in 1903 to a wealthy Jewish banking family in Hungary. Like Borel, he was a child prodigy. He enrolled at the University of Berlin in 1921, making contacts with such great names as Albert Einstein, Leo Szilard and David Hilbert. In 1926, he received his doctorate in mathematics from the University of Budapest and immigrated to the United States four years later.

In 1938, the economist Oskar Morgenstern, unable to return to his native Vienna, joined von Neumann at Princeton. He was to provide game theory with a link to a bygone era, having met the aging Edgeworth in Oxford some 13 years previously with a view to convincing him to republish *Mathematical Psychics.* Morgenstern's research interests were pretty eclectic, but centred mainly on the treatment of time in economic theory. He met von Neumann for the first time in February 1939 (Mirowski, 1991).

If von Neumann's knowledge of economics was cursory, so too was Morgenstern's knowledge of mathematics. To that extent, it was a symbiotic partnership, made and supported by the hothouse atmosphere that was Princeton at the time. (Einstein, Weyl and Neils Bohr were contemporaries and friends (Morgenstern, 1976).)

By 1940, von Neumann was synthesising his work to date on game theory (Leonard, 1992). Morgenstern, meanwhile, in his work on maxims of behaviour, was developing the thesis that, since individuals make decisions whose outcomes depend on corresponding decisions being made by others, social interaction is by definition performed against a backdrop of incomplete information. Their writing styles contrasted starkly: von Neumann's was precise; Morgenstern's eloquent. Nonetheless, they decided in 1941, to combine their efforts in a book, and three years later they published what was to become the most famous book on game theory, *Theory of Games and Economic Behaviour.*

It was said, not altogether jokingly, that it had been written twice: once in symbols for mathematicians and once in prose for economists. It was a fine effort, although neither the mathematics nor the economics faculties at Princeton were much moved by it. Its subsequent popularity was driven as much by the first stirrings of the Cold War and the renaissance of capitalism in the wake of global conflict, as by academic appreciation. It did nothing for rapprochement with Borel and his followers either. None of the latter's work on strategic games before 1938 was cited, though the minimax proof used in the book owes more to Ville than to von Neumann's own original.

In 1957, von Neumann died of cancer. Morgenstern was to live for another 20 years, but he never came close to producing work of a similar calibre again. His appreciation of von Neumann grew in awe with the passing years and was undimmed at the time of his death in 1977.

While *Theory of Games and Economic Behaviour* had eventually aroused the interest of mathematicians and economists, it was not until Duncan Luce and Howard Raiffa published *Games and Decisions* in 1957 that game theory became accessible to a wider audience. In their book, Luce and Raiffa drew particular attention to the fact that in game theory, players were assumed to be fully aware of the rules and pay-off functions of the game, but that in practice this was unrealistic. This later led John Harsanyi (1967) to construct the theory of games of incomplete information, in which nature was assumed to assign to players one of several states known only to themselves (Harsanyi & Selten, 1972; Myerson, 1984; Wilson, 1978). It became one of the major conceptual breakthroughs of the period and, along with the concept of common knowledge developed by David Lewis in 1969, laid the foundation for many later applications to economics.

Between these two great works, John Nash (1951) succeeded in generalising the minimax theorem by proving that every competitive game possesses at least one equilibrium point in both mixed and pure strategies. In the process, he gave his name to the equilibrium points that represent these solutions and with various refinements, such as Reinhard Selten's (1975) trembling hand equilibrium, it remains the most widely used game theoretic concept to this day.

If von Neumann was the founding father of game theory, Nash was its prodigal son. Born in 1928 in West Virginia, the precocious son of an engineer, he was proving theorems by Gauss and Fermat by the time he was 15. Five years later, he joined the star-studded mathematics department at Princeton – which included Einstein, Oppenheimer and von Neumann – and within a year had made the discovery that was to earn him a share (with Harsanyi and Selten) of the 1994 Nobel Prize for Economics. Nash's solution established game theory as a glamorous academic pursuit – if there was ever such a thing – and made Nash a celebrity. Sadly, by 1959, his eccentricity and self-confidence had turned to paranoia and delusion, and Nash – one of the most brilliant mathematicians of his generation – abandoned himself to mysticism and numerology (Nasar, 1998).

Game theory moved on, but without Nash. In 1953 Harold Kuhn

removed the two-person zero-sum restriction from Zermelo's theorem, by replacing the concept of best individual strategy with that of the Nash equilibrium. He proved that every n-person game of perfect information has an equilibrium in pure strategies and, as part of that proof, introduced the notion of sub-games. This too became an important stepping-stone to later developments, such as Selten's concept of sub-game perfection.

The triad formed by these three works – von Neumann–Morgenstern, Luce–Raiffa and Nash – was hugely influential. It encouraged a community of game theorists to communicate with each other and many important concepts followed as a result: the notion of cooperative games, which Harsanyi (1966) was later to define as ones in which promises and threats were enforceable; the study of repeated games, in which players are allowed to learn from previous interactions (Milnor & Shapley, 1957; Rosenthal, 1979; Rosenthal & Rubinstein, 1984; Shubik, 1959); and bargaining games where, instead of players simply bidding, they are allowed to make offers, counteroffers and side payments (Aumann, 1975; Aumann & Peleg, 1960; Champsaur, 1975; Hart, 1977; Mas-Colell 1977; Peleg, 1963; Shapley & Shubik, 1969).

The Second World War had highlighted the need for a strategic approach to warfare and effective intelligence-gathering capability. In the United States, the CIA and other organisations had been set up to address those very issues, and von Neumann had been in the thick of it, working on projects such as the one at Los Alamos to develop the atomic bomb. When the war ended, the military establishment was naturally reluctant to abandon such a fruitful association so, in 1946, the US Air Force committed $10 million of research funds to set up the Rand Corporation. It was initially located at the Douglas Aircraft Company headquarters, but moved to purpose-built facilities in Santa Monica, California. Its remit was to consider strategies for intercontinental warfare and to advise the military on related matters. The atmosphere was surprisingly un-military: participants were well paid, free of administrative tasks and left to explore their own particular areas of interest. As befitted the political climate of the time, research was pursued in an atmosphere of excitement and secrecy, but there was ample opportunity for dissemination too. Lengthy colloquia were held in the summer months, some of them specific to game theory, though security clearance was usually required for attendance (Mirowski, 1991).

It was a period of great activity at Rand from which a new rising star, Lloyd Shapley, emerged. Shapley, who was a student with Nash at Princeton and was considered for the same Nobel Prize in 1994, made numerous important contributions to game theory: with Shubik, he developed an index of power (Shapley & Shubik, 1954 & 1969); with Donald Gillies, he invented the concept of the core of a game (Gale & Shapley, 1962; Gillies, 1959; Scarf, 1967); and in 1964, he defined his 'value' for multi-person games. Sadly, by this time, the Rand Corporation had acquired something of a 'Dr Strangelove' image, reflecting a growing popular cynicism during the Vietnam war. The mad wheelchair-bound strategist in the movie of the same name was even thought by some to be modelled on von Neumann.

The decline of Rand as a military think-tank not only signalled a shift in the axis of power away from Princeton, but also a transformation of game theory from the military to the socio-political arena (Rapoport & Orwant, 1962). Some branches of game theory transferred better than others to the new paradigm. Two-person zero-sum games, for example, though of prime importance to military strategy, now had little application. Conversely, two-person mixed-motive games, hardly the most useful model for military strategy, found numerous applications in political science (Axelrod, 1984; Schelling, 1960). Prime among these was the ubiquitous prisoner's dilemma game, unveiled in a lecture by A.W. Tucker in 1950, which represents a socio-political scenario in which everyone suffers by acting selfishly, though rationally. As the years went by, this particular game was found in a variety of guises, from drama (*The Caretaker* by Pinter) to music (*Tosca* by Puccini). It provoked such widespread and heated debate that it was nearly the death of game theory in a political sense (Plon, 1974), until it was experimentally put to bed by Robert Axelrod in 1981.

Another important application of game theory was brought to the socio-political arena with the publication of the Shapley–Shubik (1954) and Banzhaf (1965) indices of power. They provided political scientists with an insight into the non-trivial relationship between influence and weighted voting, and were widely used in courts of law (Mann & Shapley, 1964; Riker & Ordeshook, 1973) until they were found not to agree with each other in certain circumstances (Straffin, 1977).

In 1969, Robin Farquharson used the game theoretic concept of strategic choice to propose that, in reality, voters exercised their franchise not sincerely, according to their true preferences, but tactically, to bring about a preferred outcome. Thus the concept of strategic voting was born. Following publication of a simplified version nine years later (McKelvey & Niemi, 1978), it became an essential part of political theory.

After that, game theory expanded dramatically. Important centres of research were established in many countries and at many universities. It was successfully applied to many new fields, most notably evolutionary biology (Maynard Smith, 1982; Selten, 1980) and computer science, where system failures are modelled as competing players in a destructive game designed to model worst-case scenarios.

Most recently, game theory has also undergone a renaissance as a result of its expansion into management theory, and the increased importance and accessibility of economics in what Alain Touraine (1969) termed the post-industrial era. However, such progress is not without its dangers. Ever more complex applications inspire ever more complex mathematics as a shortcut for those with the skill and knowledge to use it. The consequent threat to game theory is that the fundamentals are lost to all but the most competent and confident theoreticians. This would be a needless sacrifice because game theory, while undeniably mathematical, is essentially capable of being understood and applied by those with no more than secondary school mathematics. In a very modest way, this book attempts to do just that, while offering a glimpse of the mathematical wonderland beyond for those with the inclination to explore it.

Layout

The book basically follows the same pattern as the taxonomy of games laid out in Figure 1.1. Chapter 2 describes games of skill and the solution of linear programming and optimisation problems using differential calculus and the Lagrange method of partial derivatives. In doing so, it describes the concepts of utility functions, constraint sets, local optima and the use of second derivatives.

Chapter 3 describes games of chance in terms of basic probability theory. Concepts such as those of sample space, random variable and distribution function are developed from first principles and explained. Games involving risk are differentiated from those involving uncertainty, using principles such as maximin and the von Neumann utility function. Organisational characteristics such as risk aversion, risk neutrality and risk taking are also considered.

Chapter 4 digresses from the typology of games to consider sequential and simultaneous decision making. Standard means of representing sequential decision making, like directed graphs and trees, are discussed and examples are used to illustrate techniques such as the method of backward induction and optimal sub-paths, for both single-player and multi-player games. A sub-section considers the common but interesting case of single-player games involving uncertainty, the notions of a priori and a posteriori probability and Bayes's formula. The chapter finishes by considering briefly the category of games known as two-person cooperative games and the minimal social situation.

The remaining chapters consider games of strategy. Chapter 5 considers two-person zero-sum games of strategy. Games with saddle points are discussed in terms of the principles of dominance and inadmissibility, and games without saddle points are solved using mixed strategies. The solution of large matrices is considered using the notion of embeddedness and examples of interval and ordinal scales are shown to be adjustable using linear transformations.

Chapter 6 considers two-person mixed-motive games of strategy and how to represent them. The famous prisoner's dilemma game and its suggested solution in metagame theory is discussed along with three other categories of mixed-motive games without unique equilibrium points: leadership games; heroic games; and exploitation games. The Cournot, von Stackelberg and Bertrand duopoly models are fully explored, as is the solution of games without Nash equilibrium points.

Chapter 7 examines how repeated dynamic games can be analysed and how repetition itself affects outcome. Finitely and infinitely repeated games are considered, illustrated by example, and developed in the context of important concepts such as credibility, threat and discounting future pay-offs. The paradox of backward induction is also described and four theoretical methods of avoiding it are discussed.

Chapter 8 describes multi-player cooperative, non-cooperative and mixed-motive games of strategy, coalitions and the real distribution of power among voting factions on committees. Measurements of voting strength such as the Shapely value, the Shapley–Shubik, Johnston, Deegan–Packel and Banzhaf indices are described and an extended real-life example is fully explored, with some interesting results.

Finally, Chapter 9 presents a brief critique of game theory, considering the problems of rationality, indeterminacy and inconsistency, and the future role of game theory in a learning society.

Nearly 100 illustrations and 40 worked examples hopefully make this book accessible, even for those without formal mathematical training. The examples are all drawn from commonplace situations and are intended to illustrate the fundamental theoretical precepts upon which problems and conflicts are resolved, rather than the complicated reality of everyday decision making. Thus, some of the examples may appear over-simplified or a trifle contrived, but better that than the principles become obfuscated by detail, no matter how realistic. In addition, some examples are worked and then re-worked under slightly different conditions in order to present a coherent progressive study. This has the intended merit of demonstrating how subtle changes in circumstance can result in significant differences in outcome, but it has the unfortunate side effect that readers who miss the point initially, become even more confused as the story unfolds. Great care has been taken to explain these examples in the simplest terms – especially in the initial workings – to avoid the likelihood of this happening. Hopefully, the strategy has paid off and the reader's enjoyment of the book will not be curtailed by the necessity to be diligent.

2 Games of skill

It is not from the benevolence of the butcher, the brewer, or the baker, that we expect our dinner, but from their regard to their own interest.

Adam Smith 1789 'The Wealth of Nations'

Games of skill are one-player games. Since they do not involve any other player, and when they involve nature it is under the condition of certainty, they are not really regarded as genuine games. Nature does not constitute a genuine second player, as in the case of games of chance, because nothing nature does affects the outcomes of the player's choices. The solitary player in games of skill knows for certain what the outcome of any choice will be. The player completely controls the outcomes. Solving a crossword puzzle is a game of skill, but playing golf is not, since the choices that the player makes do not lead to outcomes that are perfectly predictable. Golf is a game of chance involving uncertainty, although some would call it a form of moral effort! Nature influences the outcomes to an extent which depends on the player's skill, but the probability of which is not known.

The operation of single-player decision making is discussed in the following sections. The problem of linear programming and optimisation, where a player wishes to optimise some utility function within a set of constraints, is considered with the help of some realistic examples. The application of some basic concepts from calculus, including the Lagrange method of partial derivatives, is also discussed.

Linear programming, optimisation and basic calculus

The branch of mathematics known as *linear programming* or *optimisation* is devoted to games of skill. Typically, in linear programming, the player wishes to maximise output or minimise input, given by a *utility function*, from a set of alternatives, Ω, called the *constraint* set. The player also needs to devise some criteria for ranking the alternatives in order of preference, represented by a real function:

$$f : \Omega \to \mathbb{R}$$

so that $\omega \in \Omega$ can be chosen such that $f(\omega)$ is maximised or minimised, in which case ω is known as the *optimiser* or *maximiser*.

Since optimisation involves finding the local maxima and local minima of functions (collectively called *optima*), differential calculus is often the instrument of choice for solving problems.

The *derivative* of a function $f(x)$, denoted by $f'(x)$, expresses the rate of change of the dependent variable (y) with respect to the independent variable (x). Graphically then, $f'(x)$ represents the gradient of the tangent to a curve at a particular point.

As can be seen on both Figures 2.1 and 2.2, the gradient of a tangent is zero at a maximum and a minimum. This gives us a first-order test for local optima.

If $a < p < b$ and $f'(p) = 0$, then:
If $f'(a) > 0$ and $f'(b) < 0$, then p is a local maximum;
If $f'(a) < 0$ and $f'(b) > 0$, then p is a local minimum.

The *second derivative* of a function, denoted by $f''(x)$, is the derivative of the derivative. Clearly, if the first derivative changes from positive, through zero, to negative (so that p is a local maximum), then its rate of change is decreasing. Conversely, if the first derivative changes from negative, through zero, to positive (so that p is a local minimum), then its rate of change is increasing. This gives us a second-order test for functions. It amounts to the same thing as the first-order test above, but is quicker.

If $f''(p) < 0$, then p is a local maximum;
If $f''(p) > 0$, then p is a local minimum.

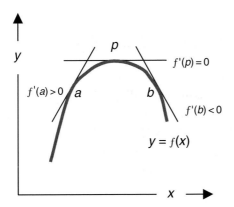

Figure 2.1   A function with a local maximum.

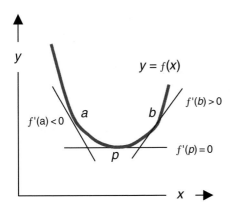

Figure 2.2   A function with a local minimum.

The following examples illustrate how the techniques are used in practice. Sometimes calculus is needed (Examples 2.2 and 2.3) and sometimes not (Examples 2.1 and 2.4).

Example 2.1 Hospital in-patient and out-patient facilities

A hospital has raised a building fund of £480 000 with which it plans to convert one of its old nurses' residences to cater for the increased numbers using the hospital.

The hospital caters for both in-patients and out-patients. Each in-patient facility (bedroom, emergency, washing and catering facilities) costs £12 000 to install. Each out-patient facility costs half that. The Hospital Trust governors want to plan the renovation so that it maximises fee income. What is the optimal balance between in-patient and out-patient facilities, and what are the implications for setting the level of fees charged to local medical practices? The fire safety and planning authorities have imposed an overall limit of 60 patients at any one time on the new facility.

Let x represent the number of out-patients accepted in the renovated 'house'. Let y represent the number of in-patients accepted.

The financial constraint imposed on the renovation can thus be expressed as:

$$6000x + 12\,000y \leq 480\,000$$

which reduces to:

$$x + 2y \leq 800$$

The constraint imposed by the planning authority can be expressed as:

$$x + y \leq 60$$

Common sense dictates that negative patients are impossible (at least in the mathematical sense!), so:

$$x \geq 0 \text{ and } y \geq 0$$

Figure 2.3 is a graphic representation of the constraint set, Ω.

Clearly, there are three possible solutions. Either the hospital plans for 40 in-patients only; or for 60 out-patients only; or for 40 out-patients and 20 in-patients.

If t is the profit per month for each out-patient and n is the profit per month for each in-patient, Figure 2.4 shows the theoretical pay-offs for each of the three strategies.

A little algebra reveals that:

• If $t > n$, then the optimal strategy is to cater for 60 out-patients only.

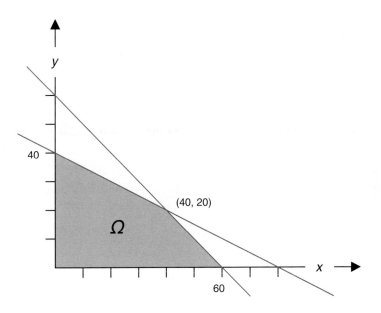

Figure 2.3 The constraint set for the conversion of a nurses' residence for in-patient and out-patient use.

		Pay-off (Profit)
		$tx + ny$
Strategy (Patient mix)	(0, 40)	$40ny$
	(40, 20)	$40tx + 20ny$
	(60, 0)	$60tx$

Figure 2.4 Pay-off matrix for the conversion of a nurses' residence for in-patient and out-patient use.

- If $n > t$, then the optimal strategy is to cater for 40 out-patients and 20 in-patients.
- If $n > 2t$, then the optimal strategy is to cater for 40 in-patients only.

Figure 2.5 puts some notional numeric values on each of these three strategies, to illustrate these features.

Profits per month

		If $t = £1600$ and $n = £1500$	If $t = £1400$ and $n = £1700$	If $t = £1000$ and $n = £2100$
	(0, 40)	£60 000	£68 000	**£84 000**
Patient mix	(40, 20)	£94 000	**£90 000**	£82 000
	(60, 0)	**£96 000**	£84 000	£60 000

Figure 2.5   Sample numerical profits for the conversion of a nurses' residence for in-patient and out-patient use.

Example 2.2 Fundraising

The Royal Ballet at Covent Garden, London, wishes to raise money by holding a series of 'popular' short matinee performances at lunchtime. The previous year, the Royal Ballet sold similar tickets for £10 each and 300 patrons attended on each of four afternoons. Experience from theatre impressarios on the Arts Council advisory board suggests that every £1 added to the price of admission results in 50 fewer people attending each afternoon; and every £1 reduction results in an increase of 50 people. If the theatre can hold anything up to 500 people, how should the ballet company pitch its pricing so as to maximise revenue?

If $(10 + x)$ represents the price of each ticket, the revenue per matinee for each of four afternoons is given by the equation:

$$R_1 = (300 - 50x)(10 + x)$$

which expands to:

$$R_1 = 3000 - 200x - 50x^2$$

Attendance is subject to the constraint:

$$300 - 50x < 500$$

which reduces to:

$$x > -4$$

The Royal Ballet seeks to maximise the R_1 revenue expression, so equating the first derivative to zero reveals any stationary point. Thus:

$$R_1' = -200 - 100x$$

has the solution:

$$x = -2$$

The second derivative confirms that this single stationary point is a maximum, since:

$R_1'' = -100$ is less than zero.

So the Royal Ballet should charge **£8 per ticket**, in which event 400 people will attend each matinee, resulting in maximum revenue of £3200 per afternoon.

Figure 2.6 is a graphic representation of the revenue function, $R_1(x)$.

It can be shown that the same pay-off would have resulted if the problem had been calculated over four shows, since:

$$R_4 = (1200 - 200x)(10 + x)$$

has the same derivative as R_1.

Example 2.3 Balancing full-time and part-time staff

A call centre in Ireland supporting IBM's voice recognition software package, 'ViaVoice', has a staffing schedule which requires 680 hours per week cover time (5 days per week; 8 hours per day; 17 lines). The staff comprises both full-time and part-time employees. The former have 20 hours per week (maximum) on-line contact, while the latter have 8 hours (maximum), and the initial staffing allocation from head office is 40 full-time equivalents. The centre currently has 30 full-time permanent employees, the minimum number required under Ireland's tax-free employment incentive scheme.

Yearly staff on-costs, which are not pro rata with the number of hours worked, are £40 per week for full-time staff and £14 per week for part-time staff. Naturally, the company wishes to minimise this overhead.

Let x represent the number of full-time staff employed at the call centre. Let y represent the number of part-time staff.

Clearly,

$$x \geq 30 \text{ and } y \geq 0$$

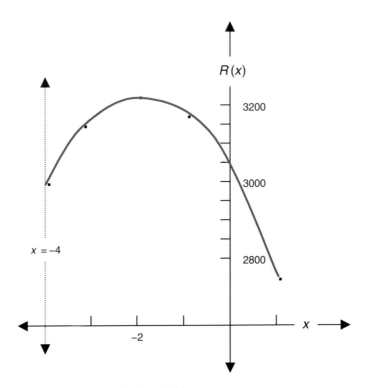

Figure 2.6   Revenue function for Royal Ballet fundraising.

and since each part-time worker (on maximum hours) is 8/20 of a full-time equivalent:

$x + 2/5y \leq 40$

Also, the minimum number of hours required per week imposes the following constraint:

$20x + 8y \geq 680$

Figure 2.7 represents the constraint set, Ω, and Figure 2.8 is a tabulation of the pay-offs for each of the four possible strategies. It can be seen that the combination of **30 full-time and 10 part-time** staff minimises the overheads.

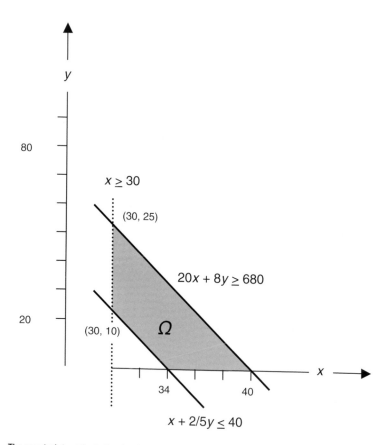

Figure 2.7   The constraint set for balancing full-time and part-time staff.

Strategy	Cost $40x + 14y$
(34, 0)	1360
(30, 10)	**1340**
(30, 25)	1550
(40, 0)	1600

Figure 2.8   Pay-offs for balancing full-time and part-time staff.

Example 2.4 Examination success and time given to tutoring

KPMG (UK), the British subsidiary of the worldwide accountancy and business services firm, has been analysing the examination results (for chartered status) of its trainees over a number of years in relation to national trends and has found that the number of hours of direct tutoring is one of the determinants of how well students do. Up to a certain point, overall results (as measured by the number of students achieving distinction grades) improve as more timetabled instruction is given, but after that, results decline as the students' practical experience diminishes.

The relationship between the number of hours timetabled per week for direct instruction (h) and the percentage by which the results are below the company's international benchmark (r), which is complicated by other variables such as age (a) and the percentage of students without a prior qualification in a numerate discipline (n), is found to be given by the equation:

$$r = \frac{n[(h-4)^{1/2} - h]}{a}$$

The company wishes to determine the optimal number of teaching hours for its trainees so as to maximise overall results, subject to a minimum requirement of 4 hours per week imposed by the Institute of Chartered Accountants code of practice.

Holding n and a constant, the derivative of r with respect to h is:

$$r'(h) = n/a[\frac{1}{2}(h-4)^{-1/2} - 1]$$

Solving the equation $r'(h) = 0$ gives:

$$\frac{1}{2}(h-4)^{-1/2} = 1$$

$$(h-4)^{1/2} = \frac{1}{2}$$

$$h = 4.25$$

Putting this result back into the equation for r gives:

$$r(h) = n/a[(0.25)^{1/2} - 4.25]$$
$$= -3.75n/a$$

In other words, the company's results are maximised at $[3.75n/a]$

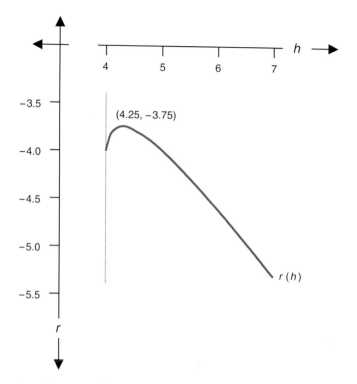

Figure 2.9   A graphic representation of the solution to the problem of examination success and the time given to direct tutoring.

below the benchmark when the number of hours per week given to direct tutoring is 4.25.

A graphic representation of the above function and its solution can be found on Figure 2.9, where the constant quotient n/a is normalised to unity for convenience.

The Lagrange method of partial derivatives

Some problems of optimisation, where the function to be optimised is a function of two variables, require a technique known as *Lagrange's method of partial derivatives* to solve them. The basic steps in the Lagrange method are as follows.

Suppose there are two functions, $f(x, y)$ and $g(x, y)$, and a new function called the *Lagrangian function*, Λ, is defined by the equation

$$\Lambda(x, y, \lambda) = f(x, y) + \lambda[c - g(x, y)]$$

where c is a constant.

The solution to the optimisation problem occurs when all partial derivatives of the Lagrangian are zero, which is analagous to the first-order test for stationary points mentioned already:

$$\frac{\delta \Lambda}{\delta x} = \frac{\delta \Lambda}{\delta y} = \frac{\delta \Lambda}{\delta \lambda} = 0$$

In other words, the following equations must be solved for x, y and λ:

$$\frac{\delta f}{\delta x} = \lambda \frac{\delta g}{\delta x}$$

$$\frac{\delta f}{\delta y} = \lambda \frac{\delta g}{\delta y}$$

$$g(x, y) = c$$

in which case all the values which produce maxima and minima for $f(x, y)$, subject to $g(x, y) = c$, will be contained in the solution set.

The following example illustrates the technique.

Example 2.5 Funding research and design

The German car manufacturer, BMW, allocates budgets internally to departmental teams on the basis of funding units for materials (M) of £25 each and production time units (T) of £60 each. The Creative Design team requires a mix of material and time units to produce an acceptable standard of project work for modelling and display.

The relationship between the number of projects modelled by the design team (S) and funding units was studied over a number of years and found to be directly proportional in the case of production time units – the more production time designers got, the greater the variety of project work produced (see Figure 2.10); and proportional to the square root of materials funding – greater funding produced greater output, but less and less so as funding increased (see Figure 2.11). Both these relationships are encapsulated in the formula:

$$S = 20 T M^{1/2}$$

Production time costs the company £40 per hour plus 50% 'on-costs' (insurance, superannuation, etc.), so each time unit is valued at £60. Each materials funding unit is valued at £25 and the Creative Design team is expected to vary the balance between the two types of funding so as to maximise project output while minimising expenditure for an expected 380 projects per week.

Let m = the number of materials funding units per week per project.
Let t = the number of time units per week per project.
Let s = the expected number of units of output = 380.
Let c = the cost of the projects per week.

Clearly,

$$c = 25m + 60t$$

and the department wishes to minimise this equation subject to the constraint

$$20tm^{1/2} = 380$$

The following three Lagrange equations must be solved:

$$\frac{\delta c}{\delta m} = \lambda \frac{\delta s}{\delta m}$$

$$\frac{\delta c}{\delta t} = \lambda \frac{\delta s}{\delta t}$$

$$20tm^{1/2} = 380$$

The partial derivatives are:

$$\frac{\delta c}{\delta m} = 25$$

$$\frac{\delta c}{\delta t} = 60$$

$$\frac{\delta s}{\delta m} = \frac{10t}{m^{1/2}}$$

$$\frac{\delta s}{\delta t} = 20m^{1/2}$$

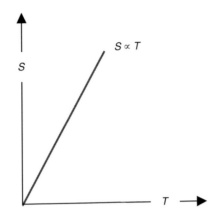

Figure 2.10 Relationship between modelling output and time units in the Creative Design department.

Substitution into the three Lagrange equations produces the following set of equations:

$$5 = \frac{2\lambda t}{m^{1/2}}$$

$$3 = \lambda m^{1/2}$$

$$20tm^{1/2} = 380$$

From the second Lagrange equation,

$$\lambda = \frac{3}{m^{1/2}}$$

Putting this into the first equation gives:

$$t = \frac{5m}{6}$$

and substituting this for t in the third Lagrange equation gives the first solution:

$$m = 8.04$$

Therefore, from the equation above,

$$t = 6.7$$

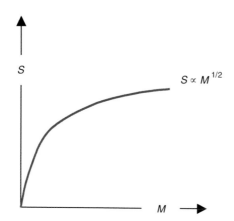

Figure 2.11 Relationship between modelling output and materials units in the Creative Design department.

and the cost per project per week is

$$c = 25(8.04) + 60(6.7)$$
$$c = \pounds 603$$

So to produce a project model, the design team should organise material expenditure of approximately £200 per week and approximately 6 hours 40 minutes per week of individual project time by staff.

3 Games of chance

Chaos umpire sits, And by decision more embroils the fray By which he reigns; next him high arbiter Chance governs all.

John Milton 1608–1674 'Paradise Lost'

Games of chance are one-player games against nature, but ones in which the single player is not making decisions under the conditions of certainty. In other words, nature affects the outcomes resulting from the player's choices in an unpredictable way. Games of chance either involve *risk*, where the probability of nature's response is known; or involve *uncertainty*, where the probability of nature's response is not known.

Those who seek to understand games of risk fully cannot but benefit from some knowledge of the concepts which underpin probability theory. It is not strictly necessary, but it is desirable. There are many outstanding texts on probability theory for readers wishing to deepen their understanding of gaming in its more esoteric forms, but the following synopsis should be sufficient for the average non-specialist reader to understand the link between game theory and the probabilistic notions of distribution function and expected value.

The following sections describe some of the underlying concepts of probability theory – probability spaces, distribution functions, random variables and expected value – as a prelude to discussing games of chance involving risk. Subsequently, utility value and games of chance involving uncertainty are considered along with the various minimax strategies used for their solution.

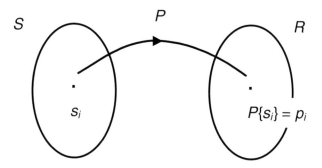

Figure 3.1   A sample space and probability of an event.

An introduction to basic probability theory

The fundamental concept in probability theory is the notion of a *probability space*. If S is a set of events called the *sample space*,

$$S = \{s_1, s_2, s_3, \ldots, s_i, \ldots, s_n\}$$

and P is a function that assigns to every subset s_i a real number $P\{s_i\} = p_i$, such that:

$$0 \leq p_i \leq 1$$

then the ordered pair (S, P) is called the *probability space* and $P\{s_i\} = p_i$ is called the *probability* of s_i (see Figure 3.1).

The *probability function*, $P(s)$, has the following six properties:
- $p_i \geq 0, \forall\, i$
- $\Sigma p_i = 1$, from $i = 1$ to n
- If $A \subset S$, then $P\{A\} = \Sigma p_i$, for all events $s_i \in A$
- $P\{\phi\} = 0$
- $P\{S\} = 1$
- If the sample space, S, is infinite, then $P(s)$ is defined only on some subset of S.

A number of other concepts flow from those given above, among them the idea of a random variable and its distribution function. A *random variable*, X, is a function mapping S onto the real numbers.

Typically, X maps an event s onto a real number $X(s)$, where $s \in S$ and $X(s) \in \mathbb{R}$. Sometimes s_i is already a real number, but other times it is not, in which case the random variable assigns one to it.

The *distribution function* of the random variable X is the function, $F(x)$, which maps the real numbers onto itself, such that:

$$F(x) = P(X), \text{ where } X \leq x, \forall\, x \in \mathbb{R}$$

In other words, the distribution function is the operation which transforms random variables into probabilities and it is the concept at the heart of many game theory solutions, as the following example illustrates.

Example 3.1

The six faces of a die have colours rather than the usual numbers. The sample space is:

$S = \{\text{red, orange, yellow, green, blue, white}\}$

The die is fair, so the probability of each outcome, $P\{s_i\} = p_i = 1/6$.

The random variable, X, assigns to each face of the die a real number. In other words, say:

$X(\text{red}) = 1,\ X(\text{orange}) = 2,\ X(\text{yellow}) = 3$
$X(\text{green}) = 4,\ X(\text{blue}) = 5,\ X(\text{white}) = 6$

The distribution function, F, is now the function that turns each random variable into a probability. In this example,

$$F(x) = P(X) = \frac{Z(s_i)}{6}$$

where $Z(s_i)$ is the number of integers less than or equal to the integer representing $X(s_i)$. So the obvious values for this distribution function are:

$F[x_{(r)}] = 1/6,\ F[x_{(o)}] = 1/3,\ F[x_{(y)}] = 1/2$
$F[x_{(g)}] = 2/3,\ F[x_{(b)}] = 5/6,\ F[x_{(w)}] = 1$

and its graph can be seen on Figure 3.2

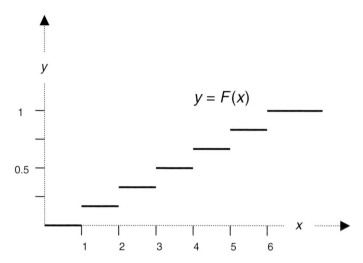

Figure 3.2   The graph of the distribution function of the random variable in Example 3.1.

This step graph is typical of the graphs of distribution functions, all of which have the following properties:

- $0 < F(x) < 1, \forall\, x \in \mathbb{R}$
- $F(x)$ is increasing
- $\lim_{x \to -\infty} F(x) = 0$, i.e. the x-axis is a barrier
- $\lim_{x \to +\infty} F(x) = 1$, i.e. the line $y = 1$ is a barrier
- $P(X) = p(x) = F(b) - F(a)$ if $a < X \le b$
- $P(X = a)$ is the jump in the distribution function $F(x)$ at $x = a$

Expected value, variance and standard deviation

Three important measurements, commonly used in statistics, are associated with random variables and their distribution functions – expected value, variance and standard deviation. In particular, expected value is the basis for solving many games of chance.

The *expected value*, $E(X)$, of the random variable X is the real number:

$$E(X) = \Sigma p_i x_i, \text{ from } i = 1 \text{ to } n, \text{ where } x_i = X(s_i)$$

In Example 3.1 above,

$$E(X) = 1/6(1) + 1/6(2) + 1/6(3) + 1/6(4) + 1/6(5) + 1/6(6)$$
$$= 3.5$$

The *variance*, $V(X)$, of the random variable X is the real number:

$V(X) = \Sigma p_i[x_i - E(X)]^2$, from $i = 1$ to n, where $x_i = X(s_i)$

Obviously, $V(X)$ is always positive.

In Example 3.1 above,

$$E(X) = 1/6[1 - 3.5]^2 + 1/6[2 - 3.5]^2 + 1/6[3 - 3.5]^2$$
$$+ 1/6[4 - 3.5]^2 + 1/6[5 - 3.5]^2 + 1/6[6 - 3.5]^2$$
$$= 2.917$$

The *standard deviation*, $\sigma(X)$, of the random variable X is the real number:

$$\sigma(X) = [V(X)]^{1/2}$$

By convention, the positive square root is taken, so $\sigma(X) \geq 0$.

In Example 3.1 above,

$$\sigma(X) = 2.917^{1/2}$$
$$= 1.708$$

For most practical game theory applications, the distribution function is usually continuous and provides enough information for a solution. The sample space and random variable are rarely used. In the case where the distribution function, $F(X)$, is continuous, it can be defined in terms of its *density function*, $f(x)$, such that:

$$F(x) = \int_{-\infty}^{x} f(x) \, dx, \forall x \in \mathbb{R}$$

The density function allows probabilities to be calculated using integral calculus, as:

$$P(X) = F(x) = \int_{a}^{b} f(x) \, dx$$
$$= F(b) - F(a), \text{ if } a < X \leq b$$

Using this new (continuous function) notation, the expected value and variance are given by the formulae:

$$E(X) = \int_{-\infty}^{+\infty} x f(x) \, dx$$

and

$$V(X) = \int\limits_{-\infty}^{+\infty} [x - E(X)]^2 f(x)\, \mathrm{d}x$$

Games of chance involving risk

A game of chance involving risk is a game in which a single player is opposed by nature. The player can assign a probability to each of nature's moves and therefore to the various outcomes of his or her own actions. Games of risk can be solved using the concept of expected value discussed above, as the following example illustrates.

Example 3.2 Funding a new high-speed rail link

Railtrack, the company that owns and manages Britain's rail structure, must accept funding for Section 2 of the new high-speed rail link from the Channel Tunnel to London (St Pancras), from one of the following bodies:
- A structural fund of the European Union (EU) makes 20 grants annually of varying amounts: three grants of £4000m; seven grants of £2000m; and ten grants of £1000m. Each year, 50 applications are shortlisted for consideration and the high-speed rail link proposal is one of them.
- A Public Transport Reconstruction Fund (PTRF), supported by the UK government and philanthropic donations from banks and businesses, makes 60 grants annually: ten grants of £2500m; 20 grants of £1500m; and 30 grants of £750m. One hundred applications are shortlisted annually and the high-speed rail link proposal is one of them.

At this stage, the Railtrack company can only proceed with one application. What are the expected values of the funding and which choice should the company make?

The figures in Table 3.1 offer the solution. The rail company should apply for EU funding, since its expected value is £720m, compared with £690m from the Public Transport Reconstruction Fund.

However, simple and attractive though this technique may be, there are a number of serious objections. In the first place, not every decision can be made on the basis of monetary value alone. If that were the case, no one would ever take part in lotteries or go to casinos since, in the long term, it is almost certain that one would lose. Even the notion of

Table 3.1 Pay-off matrix for a company applying for funding for a new high-speed rail link

Source of grant (i)	Amount of grant (£)[a] (A)	Number of such grants (G)	Probability of getting *any* grant (P)	Probability of getting *this* grant $(Q = P \times G/\Sigma G_i)$	Expected value (£)[a] $(E = Q \times A)$
EU	4000	3	0.40	$0.40 \times 3/20$	240
	2000	7	0.40	$0.40 \times 7/20$	280
	1000	10	0.40	$0.40 \times 10/20$	200
		20		**0.40**	**720**
PTRF	2500	10	0.60	$0.60 \times 5/50$	150
	1500	20	0.60	$0.60 \times 15/50$	270
	750	30	0.60	$0.60 \times 30/50$	270
		60		**0.50**	**690**

[a] Values are in millions of pounds.

insurance would be redundant, since actuaries calculate insurance premiums so as to make a profit on average. There must be something other than average monetary gain at stake when players play games.

For one thing, prudence appears to act as a counterbalance to gambling everything on the chance of a huge gain and, furthermore, there may be other than monetary values at stake in the game. For example, political pressure may be brought to bear on a company to deter it from accepting the solution with the maximum expected monetary pay-off. Or a company's creditors (numerous and influential in the case of the Channel Tunnel) may demand the safest option, irrespective of possible gain. Secondly, even in a game where the odds of winning are slightly in the player's favour, few people can afford to play the game long enough to take advantage of it. Thirdly, the size of the outcome may be an important factor and size is a relative thing. In Example 3.2, if the high-speed rail link costs £2 billion, applying to the Public Transport Reconstruction Fund makes less sense than if the rail link costs £1 billion.

Utility theory

Expected *utility* value is a better principle than expected value when it comes to guiding players through games of risk. Utility theory assumes that decisions are made on the basis of what the outcomes are worth to the player, rather than their objective value, although of course, simple pay-off value sometimes equates to utility value. Moreover, both principles share some common ground. For example, a smaller amount can never have a greater utility or pay-off value than a larger amount.

The *expected utility value* of a choice c, $U(c)$, for a continuous distribution function, is defined as:

$$U(c) = \Sigma p_i u_i, \text{ from } i = 1 \text{ to } n$$

where u_i is called the *von Neumann–Morgenstern utility function* and represents the player's preferences among his or her expected values, $E(x_i)$. In probabilistic terms, every decision involving risk is a lottery whose pay-off is the sum of the expected utility values, as the following example demonstrates.

Example 3.3 The viability of computer training courses

The City & Guilds of London Institute, the UK training organisation, offers a range of education classes in autumn and spring for adults wishing to return to work. On average, only one course in six actually runs; the others fail because of insufficient enrolment. The organisation is considering offering a new Membership diploma course (Level 6) in Information Technology, which nets the organisation £300 per capita in government capitation subsidies if it runs. At present, the organisation offers both Licentiateship (Level 4) and Graduateship (Level 5) certificate courses. The former nets it £108 per capita and the latter nets it £180 per capita.

Which course should the organisation offer – the new single diploma course (D) or the established pair of certificate courses (C) – if the organisation is: (i) risk-neutral; (ii) averse to risk; (iii) risk-taking?

The relationship between an organisation's expected utility value and its expected pay-off value can best be gauged by the manner in which it tolerates risk. There are three possibilities:

(i) the organisation is risk-neutral, in which case the relationship is:

$$u(x_i) \propto E(x_i)$$

(ii) the organisation is risk-averse, in which case the relationship is

$$u(x_i) \propto \sqrt{E(x_i)}$$

(iii) the organisation is risk-taking, in which case the relationship is

$$u(x_i) \propto E(x_i)^2$$

(i) *The organisation is risk-neutral.* The expected utility value for the 'diploma option', $U(D)$, is:

$$U(D) = 1/6(300) = \mathbf{50}$$

whereas the expected utility value for the 'double certificate option', $U(C)$, is:

$$U(C) = 1/6(180) + 1/6(108) = \mathbf{48}$$

so the diploma option is marginally preferred.

(ii) *The organisation is averse to risk.* The expected utility value for the 'diploma option', $U(D)$, is:

$$U(D) = 1/6\sqrt{300} = \mathbf{2.887}$$

whereas the expected utility value for the 'double certificate option', $U(C)$, is

$$U(C) = 1/6\sqrt{180} + 1/6\sqrt{108} = \mathbf{3.968}$$

so the certificate option is preferred.

(iii) *The organisation is willing to take risks.* The expected utility value for the 'diploma option', $U(D)$, is:

$$U(D) = 1/6(300)^2 = \mathbf{15\,000}$$

whereas the expected utility value for the 'double certificate option', $U(C)$, is

$$U(C) = 1/6(180)^2 + 1/6(108)^2 = \mathbf{7344}$$

so the diploma option is clearly preferred.

This example illustrates the point that the relationship between simple expected pay-off value and expected utility value is not necessarily linear. This agrees with most everyday experience. Doubling a sum of money, for example, may not double its utility value. (In fact, it was suggested by Bernoulli in the eighteenth century, that the most common relationship between money and utility is probably logarithmic. The utility value increases in equal steps as the corresponding cash value increases by equal proportions. For example, if £5 has a utility

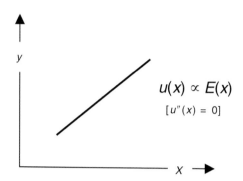

Figure 3.3   The von Neumann–Morgenstern utility function and the expected value have a linear relationship.

value of 1 and £50 has a utility value of 2, then £500 has a utility value of 3.)

The results of Example 3.3 can be represented graphically and the three categories of risk generalised to definitions, as follows:

- If the von Neumann–Morgenstern utility function, which represents a player's preferences among expected values, and the expected value itself have a linear relationship, the player is said to be *risk-neutral* (see Figure 3.3). In such a linear von Neumann–Morgenstern utility function, the player is essentially ranking the values of the game in the same order as the expected values. This, by definition, is what it means to be risk-neutral. (The values of the game in Example 3.3 are: £300 for the diploma option; and £144 for the certificate option, being the average of £180 and £108.)

  Notice that, for a linear function,

$$u''(x) = 0$$

- If the von Neumann–Morgenstern utility function is proportional to any root of the expected value, the player is said to be *risk-averse* (see Figure 3.4). Generally, risk-averse functions are of the form:

$$u(x_i) \propto \sqrt[n]{E(x_i)}$$

Notice that the derivative of a concave function such as this is clearly decreasing, so:

$$u''(x) < 0$$

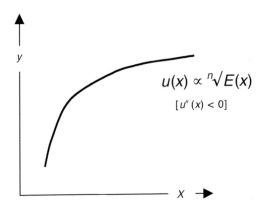

Figure 3.4 The von Neumann–Morgenstern utility function is proportional to a root of the expected value.

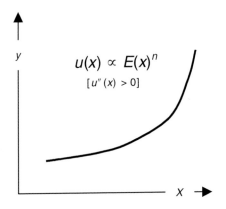

Figure 3.5 The von Neumann–Morgenstern utility function is proportional to a power of the expected value.

- If the von Neumann–Morgenstern utility function is proportional to any power of the expected value, the player is said to be *risk-taking* (see Figure 3.5). Generally, risk-taking functions are of the form:

$$u(x_i) \propto E(x_i)^n$$

and since the derivative of a convex function such as this is increasing,

$$u''(x) > 0$$

A more complicated example of the usefulness of the von Neumann–Morgenstern utility function follows.

Example 3.4 A portfolio for investment over a waiting period

Coutts, the private bank, holds £100 000 on behalf of a client in a short-term discretionary account. At the end of each year, some of the money is remitted to the client for children's school fees. For each 12-month period, the money is to be divided in some way between a portfolio of shares and a fixed-interest deposit account currently yielding 6.7% p.a.

The share portfolio yields dividends and, it is hoped, capital appreciation. It has been estimated that there is a 40% chance that the share portfolio will yield 2.4% and a 60% chance that it will yield 9.6%. How should the account manager spread the investments so as to maximise the likely return, given that the client is averse to risk on this account?

Let m represent the fraction of £100 000 invested in shares and $(1 - m)$ the fraction of £100 000 invested in fixed deposits, where $0 \leq m \leq 1$.

There is a 40% chance of getting the following return:

$$100\,000m\,\frac{102.4}{100} + 100\,000(1 - m)\,\frac{106.7}{100}$$
$$= 106\,700 - 4300m$$

There is a 60% chance of getting the following return:

$$100\,000m\,\frac{109.6}{100} + 100\,000(1 - m)\,\frac{106.7}{100}$$
$$= 106\,700 + 2900m$$

Assuming that the von Neumann–Morgenstern utility function is proportional to the square root of the expected value, the expected utility value is:

$$U(x) = 0.4(106\,700 - 4300m)^{1/2} + 0.6(106\,700 + 2900m)^{1/2}$$
$$= 4(1067 - 43m)^{1/2} + 6(1067 + 29m)^{1/2}$$

Therefore,

$$U'(x) = -86(1067 - 43m)^{-1/2} + 87(1067 + 29m)^{-1/2}$$

For a local maximum or minimum, $U'(x) = 0$, so:

$$86(1067 - 43m)^{-1/2} = 87(1067 + 29m)^{-1/2}$$
$$7396(1067 + 29m) = 7569(1067 - 43m)$$
$$m = \mathbf{0.342}$$

So the account manager should invest (approximately) 34% in the share portfolio and 66% in fixed deposits.

The second derivative verifies that $U'(x) = 0$ represents a local maximum since:

$$U''(x) = -1849(1067 - 43m)^{-3/2} - 1131(1067 + 29m)^{-3/2}$$

and, clearly, if the case of the negative root of expected value is ignored,

$$U''(x) < 0$$

Of course, any relationship between value and utility only makes sense if the pay-off is numerical – which usually means monetary. Although, in theory, it is possible to assign a utility value to any game being played, there is no reason to assume that a relationship of any kind definitely exists – linear, logarithmic, root, power or anything else. What is needed is an interval scale (a scale in which the units of measurement and the fixed points are arbitrarily, but proportionally spaced) for solving games of risk that do not have numerical outcomes. One theory, proposed by von Neumann and Morgenstern in 1944, is based on the assumption that a player can express a preference not only between outcomes, but also between any outcome and any lottery involving another pair of outcomes. The upshot of this theory is that it is possible to convert a player's order of preference among outcomes into numerical utility values. This is what makes gambling and insurance both rational games; the utility value of the gamble, involving the probable loss of a small stake for the unlikely gain of a large prize, may be positive, even if the average outcome (the cash value) over a long period of time is negative. The von Neumann–Morgenstern utility theory thus assigns arbitrary utility values to each player's least and most preferred outcomes, like the fixed points on a temperature scale. The utility values of all the outcomes in between can then be determined as follows. If the player does not differentiate between two or more outcomes, they are assigned the same utility value. Otherwise, utility values can be assigned to each outcome by comparing each outcome, like a yardstick, to a lottery involving the most and least preferred. If the player does not distinguish between a lottery with a known probability and an outcome, then that outcome can be assigned a utility value based on the same fraction of the most and least preferred values.

Utility values reflect a player's relative preferences and the von Neumann–Morgenstern theory suggests that players will always try to maximise utility value, rather than expected value, although the two may occasionally produce the same result.

Games of chance involving uncertainty

The second category of games of chance is the category of games involving uncertainty. A game of chance involving uncertainty is a game in which, like games of risk, a single player is opposed by nature, but unlike games of risk, the player cannot assign probabilities to nature's moves. Three principles for making a decision in such circumstances have been suggested and the following example illustrates all of them.

Example 3.5 Insurance against maternity leave

BNP Paribas, the French high-street bank, can take out an insurance policy to make up the shortfall between the real cost to the company of an employee on maternity leave and the entitlement under the European Union's statutory Maternity Pay Scheme. The branch managers estimate, from previous experience, that the shortfall is of the order of 10 per cent of the cost of staff cover which, including on-costs, pay-related social insurance and superannuation, comes to €13 500 per maternity leave. The insurance premium per branch is €5000 per annum. Should branches take out the insurance policy?

If a branch takes out insurance and there is no maternity cover required, then effectively the bank has lost €5000. If the branch insures and there is one case of maternity leave, the bank will still have lost €5000, but better that than losing €13 500 by not insuring! (*Note:* The bank has not gained €8500. It has still lost €5000, but is €8500 better off than if it did not insure.) Conversely, if the branch does not take out insurance and there is one case of maternity leave, it costs the bank €13 500. Of course, if the branch does not insure and there is no maternity cover required, then there is no cost involved one way or the

	Strategy	**Nature**	
		No maternity leave	1 maternity leave
Bank	Insure	– €5000	– €5000
	Do not insure	0	– €13 500

Figure 3.6   Insurance against maternity leave: pay-off matrix.

other. These four outcomes constitute the bank's pay-off matrix, which can be seen on Figure 3.6.

Of course, the pay-off matrix only shows monetary values and ignores extraneous factors such as the difficulty of getting long-term staff cover in relatively isolated rural areas or at certain times of the year.

If nature's probabilities were known to the bank, this problem would be easily solved using expected or utility values. But nature's probabilities are not known. The bank has no idea whether or not maternity cover will be required. Three suggestions for making a decision in circumstances such as these have been made: the maximax principle; the maximin principle; and the minimax principle.

The *maximax* principle recommends that the player choose the strategy that contains the greatest pay-off. It is a super-optimistic approach, comparable to the risk-taking strategy described in the previous section. It throws caution to the wind and recommends that a player choose the greatest pay-off – no matter what the downside – even when it is only marginally better than the next best strategy. The greatest pay-off on Figure 3.6 is zero, so the maximax principle tells the branch not to take out insurance.

The *maximin* principle (Wald, 1945) recommends that a player avoids the worst possible pay-off. In other words, the player should choose the strategy that offers the best worst-case scenario. This is a super-pessimistic risk-averse strategy approach and ignores the size of any possible gain no matter how large. If all game players subscribed to this principle, banks would never lend money and there would be

	Strategy	**Nature**	
		No maternity leave	1 maternity leave
Bank	Insure	€5000	0
	Do not insure	0	€8500

Figure 3.7   Insurance against maternity leave: regret matrix.

precious little research and development in industry. It can be seen from Figure 3.6 that the minimum figure on the second row is −€13 500, whereas the minimum figure on the first row is −€5000. Therefore, the worst-case scenario to be avoided is a loss of €13 500, so the other strategy should be chosen. The branch should insure.

The *minimax* principle (Savage, 1954) recommends that a player avoids the strategy of greatest regret and is a good balance between the super-optimistic and the super-pessimistic. To understand the principle, the pay-off matrix shown on Figure 3.6 must first be transformed into a *regret matrix*.

Regret matrices are constructed by calculating how much better a player could have done by choosing a different strategy if the player had known nature's choice in advance. Each pay-off in a column is subtracted from the highest pay-off in the column, to see how much better each strategy could have been. The results are shown on Figure 3.7.

Clearly the greatest regret (€8500) comes from the second row strategy – where the branch does not insure and where there is subsequently need for maternity cover – and the minimax principle suggests that this strategy should be avoided. The branch should therefore insure.

Further analysis reveals that, as long as the insurance premium is less than the benefit (€13 500), both the maximin and minimax principles will recommend taking out insurance; and the maximax principle will always recommend *not* taking out insurance, unless it is free!

4 Sequential decision making and cooperative games of strategy

To make a decision is to choose a course of action, whether in a game of skill, chance or strategy. Multiple decisions are sometimes taken simultaneously and sometimes sequentially, usually irrespective of the nature of the game, although games of skill are necessarily sequential since they involve only one player who has complete control over all the outcomes. Simultaneous decision making itself is relatively simple, although resolving the ensuing game may be difficult. Sequential decision making, on the other hand, can be very complex and certain techniques have been developed to represent the process.

This chapter considers sequential decision making in all its forms and develops the terminology used to describe directed graphs and decision making trees. The method of backward induction is illustrated by example and sequential decision making in single- and multi-player games are thus explored. The differing concepts of a priori and a posteriori probabilities are developed from a consideration of sequential decision making involving uncertainty, and Bayes's formula is used to illustrate these differences in action. The chapter concludes with a discussion on purely cooperative two-person games and the minimal social situation, which (being games without conflict) are interesting only for their decision making processes.

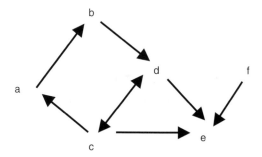

Figure 4.1 A directed graph.

Representing sequential decision making

Sequential decision making is usually represented by tree-like diagrams of various sorts. The most basic type is a *directed graph*, G_D, which is defined as an ordered pair (N, E), where N is a finite set of points called *nodes* and E is a finite set of *edges*, each of which is an ordered pairs of nodes (see Figure 4.1).

On Figure 4.1,

$N = \{$a, b, c, d, e, f$\}$
$E = \{$(a, b), (b, d), (d, c), (c, d), (c, a), (d, e), (c, e), (f, e)$\}$

For any given edge, $e = (n_1, n_2)$, n_1 is called the *predecessor* or *parent* of n_2, and n_2 is called the *successor* or *child* of n_1. On Figure 4.1, for example, d is the predecessor of both c and e.

A *path*, P, from node n_1 to node n_2 is a set of edges that start at n_1 and finish at n_2, as

$$P_{(n_1, n_2)} = \{(n_1, a), (a, b), (b, c), \ldots, (x, y), (y, z), (z, n_2)\}$$

In other words, the path joins n_1 and n_2 on the arrow diagram. n_1 is called the *ancestor* of n_2 and n_2 is called the *descendent* of n_1. On Figure 4.1, for example, the path P_{db} is

$$P_{db} = \{(d, c), (c, a), (a, b)\}$$

Eventually, of course, each path must end somewhere, since the sets of

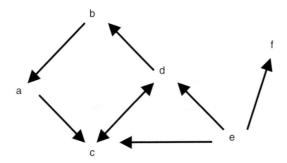

Figure 4.2   A backward directed graph.

nodes and edges are themselves finite. Such nodes are called *terminal* nodes, n_t, and are recognisable as places where edges go in, but not out. On Figure 4.1, for example, node e is a terminal node.

Conversely, every set of decisions and therefore every arrow diagram must have a starting node, called a *root*, r, which is recognisable as the node with no arrows going into it. Edges come out, but do not go in. Node f is the only root on Figure 4.1. Roots are important features of a special type of directed graphs, called a *tree*, discussed in greater detail later.

In preparation for tracing decision-making strategies back through time, from the pay-off to the root, it is worth mentioning that, for every directed graph, $G_D = (N, E)$, there exists another directed graph, $G_{DB} = (N, E_B)$, called the *backward directed graph* of G_D, whose nodes are the same as those of G_D, but whose edges are reversed. So G_{DB} for the directed graph represented on Figure 4.1, for example, is:

$N = \{a, b, c, d, e, f\}$
$E = \{(b, a), (d, b), (c, d), (d, c), (a, c), (e, d), (e, c), (e, f)\}$

and this can be seen on Figure 4.2.

As was mentioned above, a special type of directed graph exists, known as a tree, in which there is a root and (for all other nodes) one and only one path (see Figure 4.3).

It can be seen that for trees, the root is an ancestor of every node, every node is a descendent of the root and no node can have more than one parent. Also, there are no reverse paths – if there exists a path from n_1 to n_2, one does not exist from n_2 to n_1.

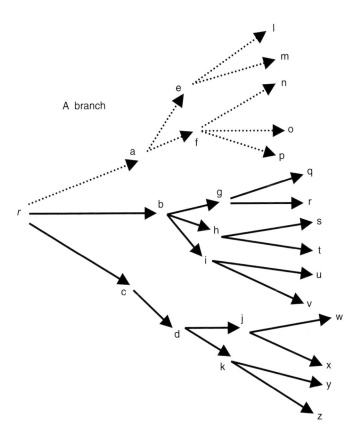

Figure 4.3   A tree, also showing a branch or sub-tree.

Trees can have *sub-trees* or *branches* (see Figure 4.3), if:
- the nodes of the branch form a subset of the nodes of the tree
- the terminal nodes of the branch form a subset of the terminal nodes of the tree
- the edges that nodes of the branch form are the same as those formed by the same nodes as part of the tree
- the root of the branch is the same node as the root of the tree.

Example 4.1 Decision tree for a proposed building programme

BGS D'Arcy, a sub-division of the advertising agency BCom3, has the option of building new premises or extending its existing facilities in Milan. Subsequent decisions must then be made, depending on which option is exercised. For example, if the agency opts for new premises on a green-field site on the outskirts of the city, it must decide whether or not to include outdoor sports facilities for staff.

Figure 4.4 represents these sequential decisions on a tree.

Sequential decision making in single-player games

A single decision maker often has to make a number of decisions in sequence and the process is best represented on a *decision-making graph*. A decision-making graph is a directed graph, like a tree but one that allows more than one path from the root to the terminal nodes which represent the pay-offs (see Figure 4.5). Every tree is a decision-making graph, but a decision-making graph is only a tree in the special case where there is only one path from the root to a terminal node.

Example 4.2 Decision graph for a system of sanction and reward

McDonald's, the chain of fast food outlets, has a recommended system of reward and sanction for its employees. Poor quality work, uncertified absence and poor punctuality not dealt with on the shop floor is referred to a shift supervisor or directly to the manager if it is serious. Sanctions range from a simple reprimand to forced redundancy.

Work or commitment likely to benefit the company is rewarded with 'merit' stars which accumulate to a promotion, a higher hourly rate of pay and end-of-year bonuses.

Figure 4.6 shows the system on a decision-making graph (not a tree!).

In a decision-making graph, if a path from n_i to n_t is optimal, then all its sub-paths must also be optimal. This is the principle upon which the *method of backward induction* is based. This is a method of tracing decisions backwards from the pay-offs at the terminal nodes, to the root. The steps for backward induction in decision-making trees are:

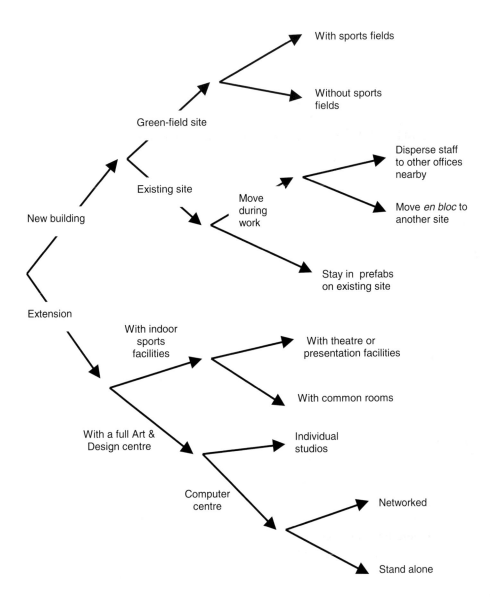

Figure 4.4 The planning process for a building programme.

- *Alpha stage*: All the parents of terminal nodes are selected and to each of these alpha nodes is assigned the best possible pay-off from their terminals. If a node has only one terminal node, then that pay-off must be assigned. All but the best pay-off nodes are deleted to get a thinned-out tree.

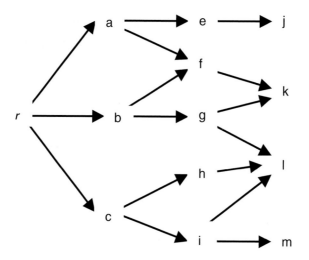

Figure 4.5   A decision-making graph.

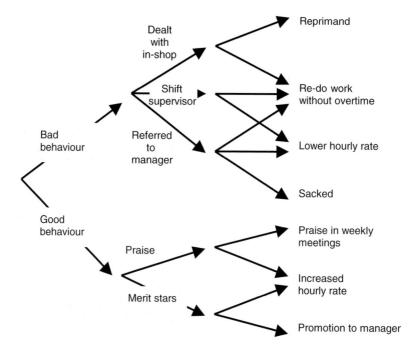

Figure 4.6   A decision-making graph for a system of sanction and reward.

The best pay-offs are not always the biggest numbers. Sometimes, in cases of minimising cost, for example, the backward selection of pay-offs is based on selecting the lowest numbers.

- *Beta stage*: The process is traced back a further step by looking at the parents of the alpha nodes – the beta nodes – and assigning to each of them the best pay-offs of their alpha nodes. Then all but the best pay-off nodes are deleted.

- *Gamma stage et seq*: The above steps are repeated to get an ever-thinning tree, until the root is the only parent left. What remains is the optimal path.

Example 4.3 Organising sponsorship

Pearson plc, the media and information company and publishers of the *Financial Times*, is considering sponsoring one of three possible events: a series of concerts or theatrical events to be held just before Christmas (proceeds to charity); an international sporting event, to be held annually in mid-October; or a literary prize to be awarded annually in March. All events involve considerable staff time, though some are more urgent than others. The company wishes to minimise the amount of staff down time and disruption involved.

Figure 4.7 (*a–e*) shows the backward induction process for the organisation of each of the three alternative events. The numbers against the tree represent the estimated number of days spent by staff in active preparation and participation.

Clearly, after all stages have been carried out, the option which involves the lowest time commitment from staff is the middle one – sponsoring the UK soccer event (50 days). The concert option involves the staff in a minimum of 64 days of preparation and participation, and the literary prize option in a minimum of 66 days of involvement.

The method of backward induction is slightly more cumbersome for decision making graphs than for trees. The pay-offs must be carried backwards in a cumulative sense, because the optimal path can only be determined when all the backward moves are made. This is a consequence of the fact that nodes may have more than one edge coming in. The following example illustrates the method.

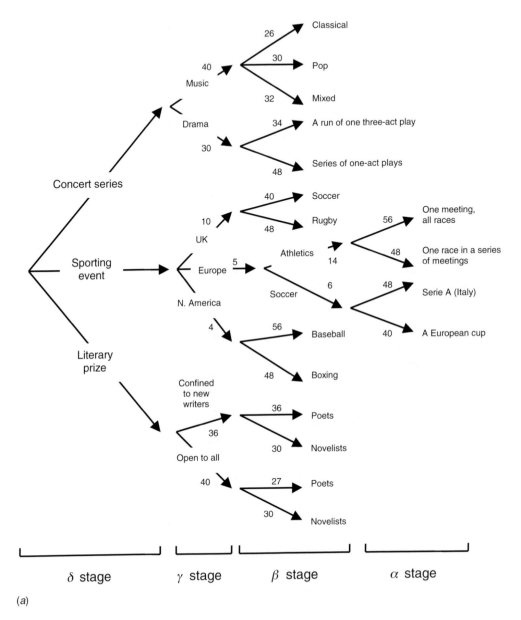

δ stage   γ stage   β stage   α stage

(a)

Figure 4.7   (a) A backward induction process for organising three sponsored events. The backward induction process after (b) the α stage; (c) the α and β stages; (d) the α, β and γ stages; and (e) all stages.

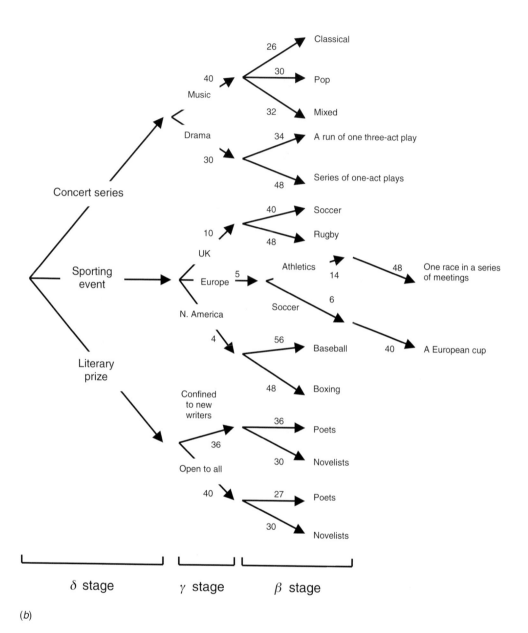

(b)

Figure 4.7 (*cont.*)

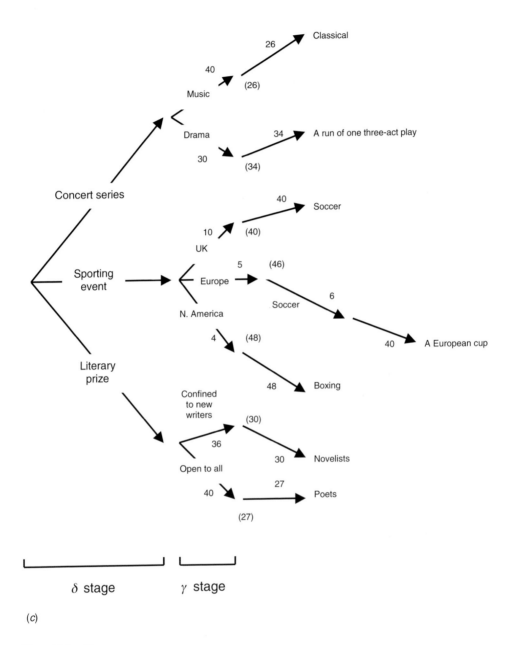

(c)

Figure 4.7 (*cont.*)

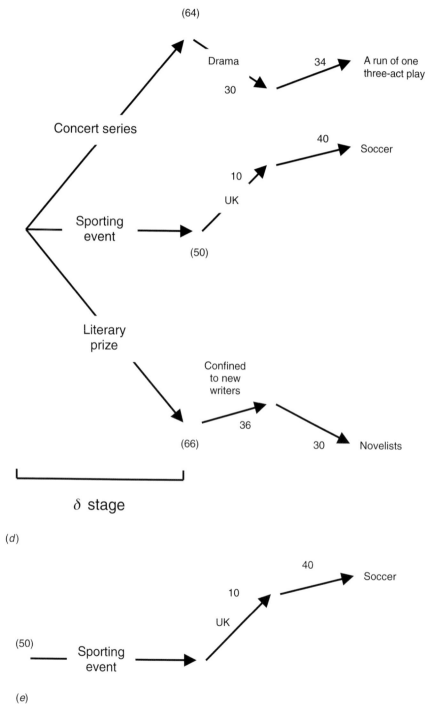

(64)

Drama — 34 → A run of one three-act play

30

Concert series

40 → Soccer

10

UK

Sporting event

(50)

Literary prize

Confined to new writers

36

(66)   30   Novelists

δ stage

(d)

40

10

UK

Soccer

(50)

Sporting event

(e)

Figure 4.7 (cont.)

Example 4.4 Appointment options

The Learning & Skills Development Agency (LSDA) needs to recruit some IT staff urgently to meet a contract for educational CD-ROMs. Figure 4.8(*a, b*) shows the method of backward induction for their recruitment process. Time is the critical factor. The agency has three appointment options: six part-time operators; four full-time programmers; or another systems manager plus two programmers. Subsequent decisions must be made about advertising the positions, convening an appointments board and checking references. The number of days involved in each step is shown beside each edge. The numbers in brackets represent backward cumulative totals. The agency needs to minimise the time for appointment.

Some nodes have more than one running total. In this event, the lowest total is selected, since the agency wishes to minimise the time to appointment. For example, there are two paths to 'Convene internal board'. One takes 21 days $(15 + 6)$ and the other takes 18 days $(10 + 8)$. It can never make sense to select the former, so it is discarded. For all calculations thereafter, this node is assigned the value 18, and the backwards process continues. The lower figure is shown in bold type on Figures 4.8, and the discarded one in light type.

The optimal strategy, as far as time is concerned, is to appoint one systems manager and two programmers by advertising internally, convening an internal appointments board and not requiring a medical examination before appointment.

Sequential decision making in single-player games involving uncertainty

In the preceding examples, it was assumed that the full consequences of each selection were known. Of course, this is not always the case in real-life situations and there is often a degree of uncertainty associated with decision making. Fortunately, there is a method for dealing with such uncertainty and that is to add nodes at which nature makes a selection in the existing tree. The following example illustrates the principle.

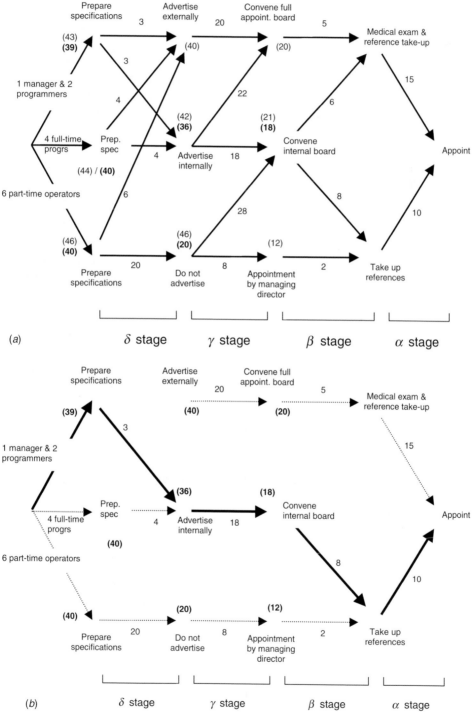

Figure 4.8 A backward induction process (*a*) for three possible appointments options, where time is the critical factor; and (*b*) after discarding from four stages and showing the optimal strategy.

Example 4.5 A university research partnership

AstraZeneca, the pharmaceutical company whose R&D division is head-quartered at Sodertajle, Sweden, was involved in a research partnership with a leading Swedish university. Unfortunately, the partnership was not successful and the agreement to collaborate lapsed. A newly appointed professor at the university wishes to revive the consortium and the company is considering how much to commit to it.

The company has decided on some involvement at least. If the company undertakes a small commitment (i.e. another company carries out the clinical trials) and it fails to produce any benefit, it will lose 150 hours of staff time. If the company undertakes a large commitment (i.e. AstraZeneca itself carries out the clinical trials) and it fails to produce any benefit, it will lose 2250 hours of staff time.

It has been estimated that success will bring 8000 or 9000 hours of free university laboratory time and professional training to the staff, depending on whether the company commits on a small or large scale, respectively.

Figure 4.9 shows the decision tree for the game. Naturally, the company wishes to maximise its benefits, although they will only accrue to the company if it continues its involvement beyond the first year, because of the longitudinal nature of the clinical trials.

The nodes marked 'chance' represent the uncertainties associated with the company's involvement; in other words, what nature does in response to the company's selected strategy. The nodes marked 'company' represent the selection of a strategy by the company.

The method of backward induction, α stage, reveals that the company should never discontinue its involvement, irrespective of its level of commitment. So the nodes marked 'company' have the values shown in brackets and the nodes marked 'chance' have the values:

$$9000p - 2250(1 - p) \text{ (upper chance node)}$$

and

$$8000q - 150(1 - q) \text{ (lower chance node)}$$

Clearly, the company will opt for large-scale involvement only when:

$$9000p - 2250(1 - p) > 8000q - 150(1 - q)$$

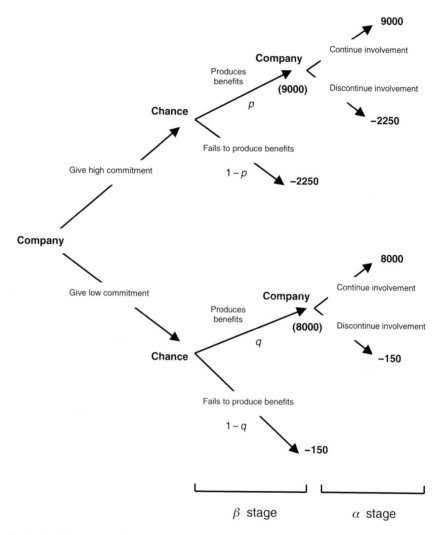

Figure 4.9   Decision tree for a company involved in a research partnership.

This condition reduces to:

$p > 0.724q + 0.186$

Interestingly, it is a consequence of this result that, even if success following small-scale involvement is certain ($q = 1$), the company should still opt for large-scale involvement as long as the probability of success following large-scale commitment (p) is greater than 0.91.

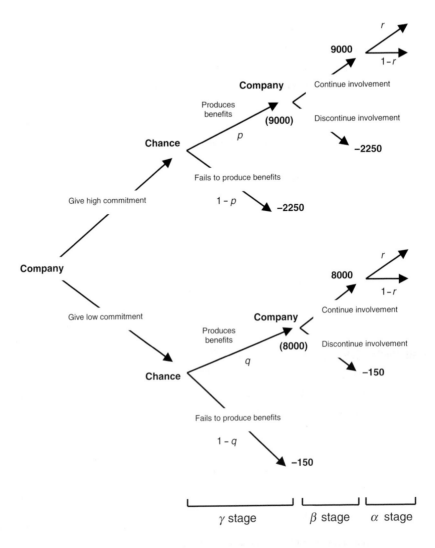

Figure 4.10 Decision tree for a company involved in a research partnership, with a priori probability.

The situation described above would be more complicated if the company was unsure of the extent to which the benefits of involvement in research would actually result in increased effectiveness within the company.

If r represents the a priori probability that the benefits (whatever they are) would result in increased effectiveness, the extended decision tree is now represented as on Figure 4.10.

There is a difference between the *a priori* probability that something will happen (denoted by r on Figure 4.10) and how this gets revised to an *a posteriori* probability when the pharmaceutical company gathers more information from experience of involvement in research or from other similar companies. The probability of one event occurring once another event is known to have occurred is usually calculated using *Bayes's formula*.

If the a posteriori probability of event A happening given that B has already happened is denoted by $p(A/B)$; and A^c denotes the complementary event of A such that:

$$p(A^c) = 1 - p(A)$$

then Bayes's formula is:

$$p(A/B) = \frac{p(B/A)\ p(A)}{p(B/A)p(A) + p(B/A^c)p(A^c)}$$

Bayes's formula is demonstrated in the following example.

Example 4.6 Schools coming out of 'special measures'

Statistics from UK government inspections of schools by Ofsted, the office for standards in education, reveal that 38% of schools in 'special measures' continue to fail after four years and are subsequently closed permanently. The preferred option for schools in special measures is to close them down, install new (sometimes private sector) management and staff, and re-open them under a new name and with enhanced resources. Some 75% of schools that eventually make it out of special measures go through this process, although 17% of the schools which were eventually closed permanently, underwent the 'close and re-open' procedure. What is the probability of success for a school in special measures after closing and re-opening?

We want to find the a posteriori probability of the school successfully passing its Ofsted inspection, given that it has undergone closure, $p(O/C)$, where O is the school passing its Ofsted inspection and C is the school undergoing closure. It is known that:

$$p(O^c) = 0.38$$
$$p(O) = 0.62$$
$$p(C/O) = 0.75$$
$$p(C/O^c) = 0.17$$

where O^c denotes the complementary event of O, i.e. the school fails its Ofsted inspection.

$$p(O/C) = \frac{p(C/O)p(O)}{p(C/O)p(O) + p(C/O^c)p(O^c)}$$

$$= \frac{0.75 \times 0.62}{0.75 \times 0.62 + 0.17 \times 0.38}$$

$$= \mathbf{0.878}$$

So schools in special measures have a 87.8% chance of passing their Ofsted inspections after closure and re-opening.

Sequential decision making in two-player and multi-player games

The discussion so far has centred on decision making by single players. The pay-offs have therefore depended only on the decisions taken by one individual (and nature, in the cases where there is uncertainty). Games which involve more than one player, but in which moves are still made one after the other, are now considered.

Multi-person sequential games can be thought of as decision-making games played in stages and, as such, they form a bridge between the decision-making theory discussed above and the 'true' games discussed in later chapters. To understand their main features, some familiar concepts need to be extended.

A tree is a *multi-player game tree* for n players if each decision node (i.e. non-terminal node) belongs to one and only one player. There should be a pay-off at each terminal node for each player (see Figure 4.11), although it may happen that some players do not own any decision nodes. (Players cannot own terminal nodes.)

The player who owns the root node (P_3) chooses a strategy (rb say) to start the game. This brings the decision-making process to another node, b, owned by another player (P_4), assuming it is not a terminal node. This player in turn chooses a strategy (bg say) which leads to node g and another player (P_1), who chooses a strategy (gk say) which leads to the terminal node, k. The pay-offs at k are, say:

4 for player P_1;   2 for P_2;   1 for P_3;   7 for P_4.

Two or more nodes of a game tree are said to be *equivalent* if:

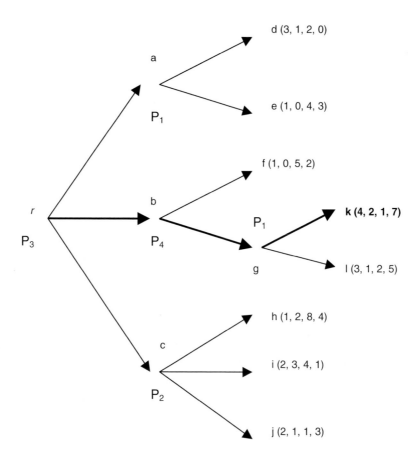

Figure 4.11   A multi-player game tree.

- they are all (m) owned by the same player;
- the same number of edges start from each, i.e. No. (E_1) = No. (E_2) = $\cdots$ = No. (E_m);
- the edges from all m nodes can be arranged in such a way that the player views them as identical. Say the edges from n_1 are:

$$E_1 = \{(n_1, \text{a}), (n_1, \text{b}), \dots, (n_1, \text{i}) \cdots\}$$

and the edges from n_2 are

$$E_2 = \{(n_2, \text{a}), (n_2, \text{b}), \dots, (n_2, \text{i}) \cdots\}$$

and the edges from n_m are

$$E_m = \{(n_m, \text{a}), (n_m, \text{b}), \dots, (n_m, \text{i}) \cdots\}$$

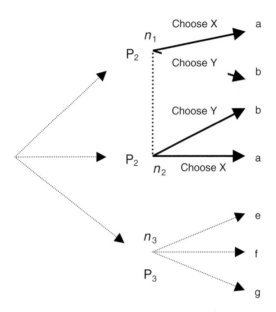

Figure 4.12   An information set for player 2.

Then this equivalence is written

$$(n_1, i) \approx (n_2, i) \approx \cdots \approx (n_m, i), \forall\ i$$

The essence of equivalence, a notion that is particularly important in games of imperfect information, is that a player cannot tell the difference between equivalent edges, since a player has no knowledge of, or cares, at what node the selection is made.

An *information set* for a player is defined as the set of all such equivalent (and therefore non-terminal) nodes belonging to the player such that no two nodes are related to one another, i.e. are not parent or child within the set. They are denoted by being joined by a dotted line (see Figure 4.12) and usually, but not always, they are all from the same stage (α, β, γ, δ, etc.).

Multi-person sequential games can now be described as multi-player game trees where decision nodes have been gathered into information sets belonging to each player. A choice for a player at a node, n, is represented by an edge coming out of n, and a *choice function* for a player who owns a set of nodes, N, is a function, f, which maps this set onto the set of its children, C:

$$f : N \rightarrow C$$

In other words, a choice function is the set of all edges coming from a player's nodes. This is the player's *strategy* – the choices that the player must make at each information set. It is a complete plan of what to do at each information set in case the game, brought by the other players, arrives at one of the information set nodes. And the set of all such strategies uniquely determines which terminal node and pay-off is reached.

As was mentioned already, sequential games can be games of either perfect or imperfect information. In the former case, each player moves one at a time and in full knowledge of what moves have been made by the other players. In the latter, players have to act in ignorance of one another's moves, anticipating what the others will do, but knowing that they exist and are influencing the outcomes. The following examples illustrate the difference.

Example 4.7 Proposing change

The newly appointed operations manager of Walmart Stores Inc., the US retail company, must decide whether or not to propose some radical changes to the way the subsidiary company, Sam's Super Centres, is managing its outlets. The board of directors must in turn decide whether to endorse these changes if and when they are made. Credibility is at stake. If the operations manager proposes changes and the board rejects them, the manager will lose considerable credibility with staff and board alike (let the ordinal pay-off for the manager for this outcome be − 2 say), although the board will remain unaffected (0). If the proposals are accepted, the manager and board both gain, but the former (+ 2) more than the latter (+ 1), since the manager initiated them.

The tree for this game is shown on Figure 4.13. The pay-offs are ordinal in the sense that they represent the ranking of preferred outcomes only, without scale. (The manager's pay-offs have been shown first in the ordered pairs.)

The game is clearly one of perfect information. Both players know precisely the nodes where they must make choices, so each player knows all the previous choices that have been made.

It is noticeable that every information set has only one element and, in fact, this is true for all games of perfect information – a game will be

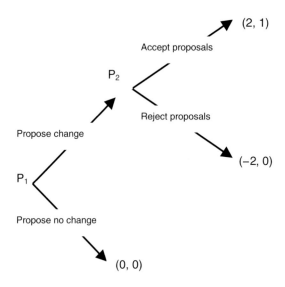

(*The manager's pay-off comes first in the ordered pair.*)

Figure 4.13   Proposing change: a game of perfect information.

one of perfect information if every information set has only one element. Otherwise, the game will be one of imperfect information, as the following example shows.

Example 4.8 Proposing change under uncertainty

Suppose in the situation outlined in the previous example (Example 4.7), the board of directors had already been approached by the Sam's Super Centres' regional manager who wished to take early retirement on health grounds. The board then made its decision in relation to the regional manager but, upon request, did not make the new operations manager aware of it before the latter had made her recommendations for change.

This game can be represented as a three-player game – the third player being nature, which has decided whether or not the grounds for ill-health retirement are sufficiently strong (see Figure 4.14).

The ordinal pay-offs shown on Figure 4.14 are explained as follows. If the board has not accepted the regional manager's retirement, the pay-offs revert to those of Example 4.7 (bottom half of Figure 4.14). If

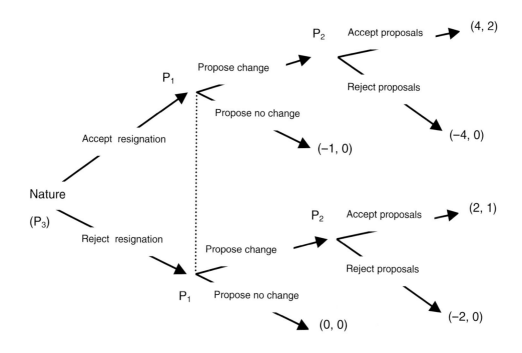

(*The manager's pay-off comes first in the ordered pair.*)

Figure 4.14   Proposing change under uncertainty: a game of imperfect information.

the board has accepted the retirement, unbeknown to the new operations manager, and she proposes no change, then the manager loses some credibility with staff (-1) and there is no alteration in the status of the board (0). If, under the same circumstances, the operations manager proposes change and the proposals are accepted by the board, the manager gains massively ($+4$) and the board gains to a lesser extent ($+2$) for their foresight and flexibility. However, if the board rejects the proposals for change, notwithstanding the regional manager's resignation, the operations manager will appear out-of-touch and unsympathetic (-4), while the board will at least appear sympathetic in the eyes of staff ($+1$).

In this game, the operations manager cannot distinguish between the two nodes in her information set. There is more than one node in the information set, so the game is one of imperfect information. The operations manager, at the time of making her choice, does not know of nature's outcome, although the board, making its decision after her, does.

Cooperative two-person games

Cooperative two-person games are interesting only for their decision-making processes, since they are games without conflict in which the players have coinciding interests. In fact, some writers on game theory (Luce & Raiffa, 1989) have suggested that purely cooperative games are not games at all in the true sense, since both players have a unitary interest and may therefore be regarded as a single playing entity.

There are two classes of cooperative two-person games: purely cooperative games, where the interests of both players coincide perfectly; and minimal social situation games (Sidowski, 1957), which are characterised by ignorance on the players' part as to their own strategic interdependence, although it is still in their interests to cooperate. Purely cooperative games may be games of perfect or imperfect information, but minimal social situation games are necessarily ones of imperfect information.

In a purely cooperative game, it is in each player's interest to anticipate the other player's selection so that a mutually beneficial outcome can be obtained. Each player knows that the other is similarly motivated. This feature is absent from minimal situation games, either through lack of communication or lack of understanding about the rules, although it is still in the players' mutual interest to cooperate.

Purely cooperative games

In purely cooperative games, both players must agree on their order of preference of possible outcomes, so that there is no conflict of interest. This is their incentive for cooperating – that they achieve an outcome which they both prefer. The games can be ones of either perfect or imperfect information. In some games, players may be able to anticipate the strategies others will choose, if all players know the rules of the game and the preferences of the other players (complete information). In other games, where the condition of complete information does not apply, no unique best combination of strategies exists and a solution must be sought through informal analysis.

It has been shown (Schelling, 1960) that informal analysis often reveals a focal point which possesses a certain prominence. Even if the players cannot communicate explicitly with one another, there is always the chance that each will notice the focal point and assume that the other has noticed it too as the obvious solution. For example, in the case of the two cyclists on the path heading towards one another, the focal point might be the UK traffic regulation: 'road users must drive on the left'. Each cyclist would therefore assume that the other would use this rule as a basis for choosing, and so each would choose accordingly. The rule acts like a beacon and decision making tends towards it. Such focal points may be rooted in national, local or institutional culture and when they are, they are all the more pre-eminent for that.

Minimal social situation games

The *minimal social situation* is a class of games of imperfect information, where the players are ignorant of their own pay-off functions and the influence of other players. Each player only knows what choices may be made. In some minimal situation games, one player may not even know of the existence of the others.

Kelley et al. (1962) proposed a principle of rational choice for minimal social situation games known as the '*win–stay, lose–change*' principle. This principle states that, if a player makes a choice which produces a positive pay-off, the player will repeat that choice. On the other hand, if a player makes a choice which produces a negative pay-off, the player will change strategy. Thus, strategies which produce positive pay-offs are reinforced and ones which produce negative pay-offs are not.

Again, the distinction must be made between players in a minimal social situation game making decisions simultaneously and those in which decisions are made sequentially. The following two examples illustrate the significant differences in outcome that can result from these subtle differences in process.

Kelley, Drye & Warren LLP

Strategy	Supplier A	Supplier B
Supplier A	2 content; 1 content	2 content; 1 discontent
Supplier B	2 discontent; 1 content	2 discontent; 1 discontent

Clifford Chance LLP (row player)

Choosing supplier A makes the other player content, whereas choosing supplier B has the opposite effect

Figure 4.15   Dealing with suppliers.

Example 4.9 Dealing with suppliers: acting successively

Each year, two New York commercial law firms, Clifford Chance LLP and Kelley, Drye & Warren LLP, choose between two companies (A and B) who supply stationery and office supplies. Successive decisions are made by each of the firms' two principal legal secretaries. If either law firm selects supplier A, then the other is made content because supplier A showers them with special offers in an attempt to get their business also. (Supplier A enjoys an economy of scale if it services both firms, since both are on Park Avenue.) If either firm chooses supplier B, then the other is made discontent, because certain special offers are withdrawn.

Figure 4.15 shows the pay-off matrix.

Analysis reveals three distinct sequences.

- Say Clifford Chance chooses supplier A first and Kelley, Drye & Warren follows by choosing supplier A too. The series of decisions looks like this:

  A − A, A − A;   A − A, etc.

- If Clifford Chance chooses B first and Kelley, Drye & Warren follows by choosing supplier B too, both become discontent. So the former changes, thus rewarding the latter who naturally sticks with the original strategy. Still receiving no satisfaction, Clifford Chance changes again, which makes Kelley, Drye & Warren discontent, and it now changes to supplier A. Clifford Chance is now content and sticks with B, making Kelley, Drye & Warren discontent and causing another change. The whole cycle repeats itself endlessly and the series of decisions looks like this:

B − B, A − B, B − A;   B − B, etc.

- If Clifford Chance chooses supplier A and Kelley, Drye & Warren subsequently chooses supplier B, analysis reveals that the pattern looks like this:

A − B, B − A, B − B;   A − B, etc.

If Clifford Chance chooses Supplier B and Kelley, Drye & Warren subsequently chooses A, analysis reveals that the pattern looks like this:

B − A, B − B, A − B;   B − A, etc.

Both cycles repeat themselves endlessly without ever achieving the stability of mutually favourable outcomes.

Example 4.10 Dealing with suppliers: acting simultaneously
Now consider the same case, but where the law firms make their selections not successively, but simultaneously, unaware of the other's choice.

Analysis reveals that:
- If both firms randomly choose supplier A, both will receive favourable outcomes, and so both will stay with their selections. The series of decisions will look like this:

AA − AA − AA − AA, etc.

- If both firms randomly choose supplier B, both will receive unfavourable outcomes and both will change their original strategies. In this case, the series of decisions will look like this:

BB − AA − AA − AA, etc.

- If Clifford Chance chooses supplier A and Kelley, Drye & Warren simultaneously chooses supplier B, the former will be discontent and change to B next time. The latter will be content with the first choice and so stick with it. Each firm will now become discontent and change. The series of decisions will look like this:

AB — BB — AA — AA, etc.

A similar series emerges when Clifford Chance chooses B and Kelley, Drye & Warren simultaneously chooses A.

Two conclusions may be drawn from this analysis of simultaneous decision making. The first is that the decision-making process will eventually settle down and achieve stability around the outcome that makes both players content (AA). The second conclusion is that, unless players hit on the right combination first time, they must pass through a mutually unsatisfactory outcome (BB) before they can achieve stability around the mutually satisfying one (AA).

A comparison between the two examples reveals that sequential decision making in cooperative games differs significantly from simultaneous decision making. For one thing, the series of strategic selections does not inevitably lead to a mutually rewarding conclusion. In fact, the sequential selection of strategies *never* leads to stability. It just goes round and round endlessly, which is just about the worst-case scenario for any management team!

Admittedly, minimal social situation scenarios are a trifle contrived. In most realistic situations, players are not unaware of their mutual interdependence, so strictly minimal social situations are very rare. Players are usually informed of each other's existence and realise that their choices influence each other's pay-offs, although it is common enough that players do not fully understand the pay-off structure.

5 Two-person zero-sum games of strategy

He either fears his fate too much, Or his deserts are small, That puts it not unto the touch to win or lose it all.

James Graham, Marquess of Montrose 1612–1650 'My Dear and only Love'

A two-person zero-sum game is one in which the pay-offs add up to zero. They are strictly competitive in that what one player gains, the other loses. The game obeys a *law of conservation of utility value*, where utility value is never created or destroyed, only transferred from one player to another. The interests of the two players are always strictly opposed and competitive, with no possibility of, or benefit in, cooperation. One player must win and at the expense of the other; a feature known as *pareto-efficiency*. More precisely, a pareto-efficiency is a situation in which the lot of one player cannot be improved without worsening the lot of at least one other player.

Game theory is particularly well-suited to the analysis of zero-sum games and applications to everyday life (especially sporting contests) abound. Actually, 'constant-sum games' would be a better title since, in some circumstances, the pay-offs do not add up to zero because the game is unfair. However, they do sum to a constant, which is the prevalent feature of these strictly competitive games, so we will continue to use the term 'zero-sum' even in these instances, for the sake of simplicity.

The section that follows establishes a link between the tree representation described in the previous chapter and the normal form of the game, represented by pay-off matrices. Subsequent sections describe various methods for solving games with and without saddle points and show how the issue of security leads inexorably to the notion of mixed strategy. The chapter concludes with a discussion of interval and ordinal scales and shows that game theory analyses can recommend strategies even in cases where specific solutions cannot be found.

Representing zero-sum games

There are two classes of zero-sum games – finite and infinite. Finite zero-sum games are those in which both players have a finite number of pure strategies. Infinite zero-sum games are those in which at least one player has an infinite number of pure strategies from which to choose and are thankfully fairly rare. Only some infinite games have solutions, but all finite ones do. A *solution* to a zero-sum game is a specification of the way each of the players should move. If both players move according to this specification, then the pay-off that results is known as the *value* of the game.

Two-person zero-sum finite games are usually represented using pay-off matrices, but in order to demonstrate the link with game trees and decision making, Figure 5.1 shows the game in tree form.

As usual, the terminal nodes of the game tree represent the outcomes and joining nodes – here with a dotted line – indicates an information set. When making a move, a player cannot distinguish between nodes in an information set. If the game is one of imperfect information, where the players move in ignorance of any previous moves, the player must choose without knowing what the other player has simultaneously chosen. In a game of perfect information, on the other hand, the nodes on the game tree will all be individual information sets (see Figure 5.2).

Figure 5.3 is the pay-off matrix representation for the same game, sometimes called the *normal form* of the game. Each row corresponds to a pure strategy for player 1 and each column corresponds to a pure strategy for player 2. The matrix element at the intersection of a row and a column represents, by convention, the pay-off to the row player. The column player's pay-offs will be the negatives of those shown on the matrix.

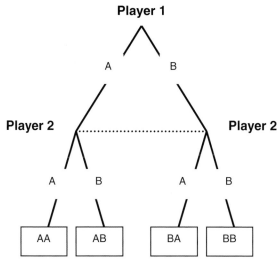

Figure 5.1   Game-tree diagram for a two-person zero-sum game of imperfect information.

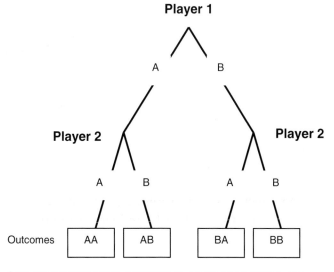

Figure 5.2   Game-tree diagram for a two-person zero-sum game of perfect information.

Player 2

Strategy	Strategy A	Strategy B
Player 1 Strategy A	AA	AB
Strategy B	BA	BB

Figure 5.3   A pay-off matrix for a two-person zero-sum game.

Games with saddle points

How does the row player analyse the pay-off matrix in order to select the optimal strategy? One option is to use the maximin principle, where the player chooses the strategy which contains the best of the worst possible outcomes. In other words, the player chooses to maximise the minima and so guarantee that the pay-off will not be less than a certain value – the row player's *maximin value*.

Of course, the column player is making a strategic decision using the same logic. Since the pay-off matrix shows the pay-offs for the row player, the column player is trying to minimise the row player's maxima. In other words, the column player is adopting a minimax principle.

The two strategies – the row player's maximin strategy and the column player's minimax strategy – may or may not coincide. If they do, the game has a *saddle or equilibrium point,* which represents the pay-off that results from best play by both players (see Figure 5.4). The players can only do worse, never better, by selecting anything other than the optimal saddle point strategy – it is the outcome that minimises both players *regret.*

Since the saddle point represents the row player's maximin and the column player's minimax, it can always be found as the element that is a minimum in its row and a maximum in its column. All finite zero-sum games with perfect information have at least one saddle point. In fact, the condition of perfect information itself is sufficient to ensure a saddle point, even for games that are too complex to solve or even to represent diagrammatically (Zermelo, 1913).

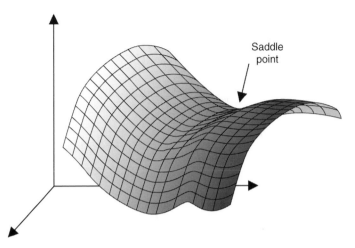

Figure 5.4   A saddle point.

	Player 2		
Strategy	**A**	**B**	**C**
A	5	2	3
Player 1 **B**	8	2	4
C	3	1	2

Figure 5.5   A pay-off matrix with two saddle points.

Sometimes saddle points are unique and there is only one for the game. Other times there is no saddle point or there are multiple ones. Games without saddle points require fairly complicated methods to find a solution and are discussed later, but games with multiple saddle points present no new problems. Figure 5.5 shows a pay-off matrix with two saddle points. The solution for player 1 is to choose either strategy A or strategy B. The solution for player 2 is simply to choose strategy B.

The following examples illustrate the methods by which two-person zero-sum games may be represented and how they may be solved.

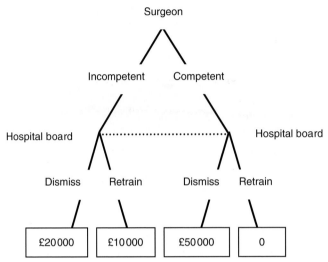

Figure 5.6   Game-tree diagram for professional incompetence: retain and retrain.

Example 5.1 Medical incompetence: retain and retrain?

A hospital ethics committee in the UK has assessed a surgeon as falling short of the level of care and competence demanded of professionals in that field. The surgeon disputes this and has received advice from the appropriate professional association. The surgeon has two options: to accept the committee's assessment (incompetence) or to reject it (competence). The hospital board has two options; to dismiss the surgeon with a redundancy package, or to retain and retrain the surgeon. Both surgeon and hospital must make submissions to the General Medical Council (the licensing and disciplinary body for the medical profession in the UK) and the government Department of Health in writing, by the same date, declaring their positions for arbitration.

Figure 5.6 shows a game tree for the game.

The game is one of imperfect information. Each player must choose without knowing what the other has decided, so the two nodes representing the hospital board's strategy are shown joined together by a dotted line. The terminals represent the outcomes of the different strategies. If the surgeon accepts the committee's assessment (declared incompetent), retraining will cost the hospital £10 000. There will obviously be no retraining cost if the surgeon is declared competent. If the surgeon is dismissed and declared incompetent, it will cost the hospital £20 000 in redundancy. If the surgeon is dismissed and yet

Hospital board

Strategy	Dismiss with retirement package	Retain & retrain
Surgeon Accept incompetency assessment	£20 000	£10 000
Reject incompetency assessment	£50000	0

Figure 5.7   Pay-off matrix for professional incompetence: retain and retrain.

declared competent, it will cost the hospital an estimated £50 000 in compensation.

Figure 5.7 shows the pay-off matrix for the game. Clearly, the surgeon's maximin strategy (£10 000) is to accept the committee's assessment. The hospital board's minimax strategy (also £10 000) is to retain and retrain the surgeon. This is therefore a unique saddle point for the game. Neither the surgeon nor the hospital board can do better by choosing any other strategy.

Example 5.2 Reforming a travel timetable

Pacific Western, one of the bus operating companies for Pearson Airport, Toronto, operates a 21-hour week for its drivers. The operations manager is restructuring the travel timetable to the airport, offering new routes and fewer stops, and he has three models in mind. One is based on twenty 63-minute journeys; another on twenty-one 60-minute journeys; and a third model based on twenty-eight 45-minute journeys (dubbed the 'Airport Rocket'). At the same time, the personnel manager is considering whether to employ four, five or six bus drivers on the airport run.

To meet the terms of a binding legal agreement with unions and the General Toronto Airport Authority, all bus drivers must receive the same weekly employment at a fixed rate, so some arrangements provide drivers with off-the-road time – which can be filled with clerical and maintenance duties - while others do not. Table 5.1 shows the balance of driving and off-road periods for each of the nine strategies.

The personnel manager, choosing the number of drivers, wishes to maximise driving time. The operations manager, choosing the travel schedule, wishes to minimise it to keep more flexibility for other (shorter) routes and indirectly keep maintenance and secretarial staffing to a minimum.

Table 5.1 Nine configurations for reforming a travel timetable

Weekly timetable	No. bus drivers	No. journeys per driver	No. off-the-road periods	Driving time (h/m)
20 × 63-min journeys	4	5	0	21/0
	5	4	0	21/0
	6	3	2	18/54
21 × 60-min journeys	4	5	1	20/0
	5	4	1	20/0
	6	3	3	18/0
28 × 45-min journeys	4	7	0	21/0
	5	5	3	18/45
	6	4	4	18/0

	Operations manager		
Strategy	**20 journeys**	**21 journeys**	**28 journeys**
4 drivers	21	**20**	21
5 drivers	21	20	18 / 45
6 drivers	18 / 54	18	18

(Personnel manager — rows)

Figure 5.8   Pay-off matrix for reforming a travel timetable.

Figure 5.8 shows the pay-off matrix for the game.

The saddle point is the element that is minimum in its row and maximum in its column and this occurs when the timetable has 21 journeys per week and four drivers. The value of the game is thus 20 hours.

This technique for finding maximum saddle point solutions is a useful one for very large matrices (see Figure 5.9). Each row minimum can be examined in turn, to see which, if any, is also a maximum in its column.

Player 2

		a	b	c	d	e	f	g
	a	6	7	5	11	8	12	10
	b	14	12	12	11	10	12	13
	c	10	7	8	13	4	10	9
Player 1	d	8	4	2	13	8	14	10
	e	13	7	8	14	5	14	10
	f	12	9	8	13	9	12	8
	g	10	7	3	14	7	14	10

Figure 5.9   A large matrix with a saddle point.

Strategy	Column 1	Column 2
Row 1	*a*	*b*
Row 2	*c*	*d*

Figure 5.10   Dominance and admissability.

Figure 5.9 is a seven-by-seven matrix and closer inspection reveals a saddle point at row b, column e, where the value of the game is 10. In a zero-sum game, since the pay-off for one player is the negative of the pay-off for the other, a game is said to be *fair* if the value of the game is zero. None of the games we have considered so far has been fair in that sense. In the case of the surgeon charged with incompetence, the game is unfair because the surgeon cannot ignore the allegation. In the case of the new Toronto Airport bus timetable, the game is unfair because not changing the timetable is not an option.

Dominance and inadmissibility in large saddle point games

Sometimes one of a player's pure strategies *dominates* the other ones in that it yields an outcome at least as good against any strategy that the opposing player may select. It cannot make sense for a rational player to select a dominated strategy and it is thus said to be *inadmissible.* More formally, one row dominates another when elements in the dominant row are larger and as large (smaller in the case of dominant columns) as the corresponding elements in the inadmissible row. For example, in Figure 5.10, row 1 dominates row 2 if $a > c$ and $b \geq d$, for all $a, b, c, d \in \mathbb{R}$.

Player 2

Player 1		b	c	d	e		g
b		12	12	11	**10**		13
d		4	2	13	8		10
e		7	8	14	5		10
f		9	8	13	9		8
g		7	3	14	7		10

Figure 5.11 First elimination of dominated rows and columns.

The notions of dominance and inadmissibility provide an alternative method to the minimax/maximin strategy for locating saddle points. Consider Figure 5.9 again. Row c is dominated by row e (higher numbers everywhere) so there is no reason why player 1 should ever select it. Similarly, row a is dominated by row b. Once row a has been eliminated, column a is dominated by column b (lower numbers everywhere) so there is no reason why player 2 should ever select it. Similarly, column f is dominated by column e. These four eliminations reduce the matrix to the five-by-five matrix shown in Figure 5.11.

Four further eliminations reduce Figure 5.11 to a three-by-three matrix. Column d is dominated by column e. Once column d is gone, row e is dominated by row f and row d is dominated by row b. Once row e is gone, column b is dominated by column c. The matrix has now been reduced to the three-by-three matrix shown in Figure 5.12.

Another four eliminations produce the unique saddle point at row b, column e (see Figure 5.13).

While this method of eliminating inadmissible rows and columns to produce a saddle point eventually is cumbersome and certainly not as immediate as the minimax strategy (where the saddle point is the element which is minimum in its row and maximum in its column), it is useful in that it demonstrates why a game of perfect information can always be solved.

Games with no saddle points

Some two-person zero-sum games have no saddle point and are relatively complicated to solve.

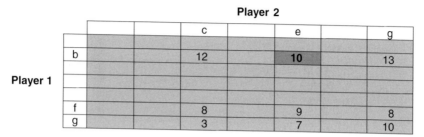

Player 2

			c		e		g
b			12		**10**		13
f			8		9		8
g			3		7		10

Figure 5.12   Second elimination of dominated rows and columns.

Player 2

					e		
b					**10**		

Figure 5.13   Final elimination of dominated rows and columns.

Example 5.3 Re-allocation of duties

The trade union representing airline pilots in Germany (Vereinigung Cockpit e.V.) and that representing cabin crews (Unabhangige Flugbegleiter Organisation, UFO) are in conflict with each other over a possible reallocation of duties at Lufthansa, the German airline. Each group has been given the opportunity to change to a new rota either immediately or subsequent to proposals for a redistribution of duties among airline staff made by representatives of the cabin crews.

The pilots and cabin crews potentially stand to gain (or lose) a performance related bonus from Lufthansa, depending on what they choose to do. If both groups change simultaneously, the pilots will gain nothing since it will be perceived that they are blindly following the leadership shown by their more junior colleagues. The cabin crews will gain everything since it was their initiative. However, if the pilots change first and the cabin crews later, the pilots will gain, since it will be assumed that it was they who took the lead. If the cabin crews change now and the pilots change later, credibility and the performance related bonus will probably be shared, with approximately 75% going to the cabin crews.

		Cabin crews (UFO)	
	Strategy	Change now	Change later
Pilots (Cockpit e.V.)	Change now	0	100%
	Change later	25%	0

(Pay-offs for the row player only are shown)

Figure 5.14   Pay-off matrix for two groups in conflict over re-allocation of duties.

Figure 5.14 shows the pay-off matrix for the game. Clearly, the game is an imperfect one and has no saddle point, since there is no element in the matrix which is a row minimum and a column maximum. Such matrices are not unusual and the larger the matrix, the more likely it is that it will not have a saddle point. However, it is still possible to find a rational solution.

If the groups try to out-guess each other, they just go round in circles. If the pilots use the minimax principle, it makes no difference whether they change now or later – the minimum gain is zero in either case. The cabin crews will attempt to keep the pilots' gain to a minimum and will therefore opt to change now. The most that the pilots can gain thereafter is 25% of the performance bonus. However, the pilots can reasonably anticipate the cabin crew strategy and will therefore opt to change later to guarantee themselves 25%. The cabin crews can reasonably anticipate this anticipation and will consequently opt to alter their choice to 'later', thereby keeping the pilots' gain to zero. This cycle of counter-anticipation can be repeated *ad nauseam.*

There is simply no combination of pure strategies that is in equilibrium and so there is no saddle point. All that can be said is that the value of the game lies somewhere between zero and 25%. One of the groups will always have cause to regret its choice once the other group's strategy is revealed. A security problem therefore exists for zero-sum games with no saddle point. Each group must conceal their intentions from the other and, curiously, this forms the basis for a solution.

The best way for players to conceal their intentions is to leave their selections completely to chance, assigning to each choice a predetermined probability of being chosen. This is called adopting a *mixed*

	Strategy	Cabin crews (UFO)		Probability
		Change now	Change later	
	Change now	0	100%	$p = 0.2$
Pilots (Cockpit e.V.)	Change later	25%	0	$1-p = 0.8$
	Probability	$q = 0.8$	$1-q = 0.2$	

(*Pay-offs for the row player only are shown*)

Figure 5.15 Pay-off matrix for the re-allocation of duties, with assigned probabilities.

strategy. Mixed strategies that are in equilibrium, where neither player can profit by deviating from them, give rise to strategies called *minimax mixed strategies*. Such strategies are optimal in that they are the best strategies available to rational players and, along with the value of the game, constitute the solution. In a sense, games that have saddle points are simply special cases of mixed-strategy games, in which a probability of zero is assigned to every selected strategy except one, which is assigned a probability of unity. This is a consequence of von Neumann's fundamental minimax theorem (1928), which states that every finite strictly competitive game possesses an equilibrium point in mixed strategies. (A proof of the minimax theorem can be found in Appendix A.)

The game represented in Example 5.3 can thus be solved by assigning probabilities as follows (see Figure 5.15). Let the pilots' first-row mixed strategy be assigned a probability p and the second-row mixed strategy a probability $1 - p$. Since the game is zero-sum, the expected pay-offs yielded by the two strategies are equal. Therefore:

$$0(p) + 25(1 - p) = 100(p) + 0(1 - p)$$

which gives the solutions:

$$p = 0.2 \text{ and } 1 - p = 0.8$$

Similarly, let the cabin crews' first-column mixed strategy be assigned a probability q and the second-column mixed strategy a probability $1 - q$. Again, the expected pay-offs yielded by these two strategies are equal. Therefore:

$$0(q) + 100(1 - q) = 25(q) + 0(1 - q)$$

which gives the solutions:

$q = 0.8$ and $1 - q = 0.2$

The pilots should therefore choose the first strategy ('change now') once in every five random selections and choose the second strategy the other four times. Conversely, the cabin crews should choose to 'change now' four times in every five random selections and choose to 'change later' on the other occasion.

The groups can choose whatever method they like for randomising the selection of their strategies. For example, one of the pilots may have five different denomination coins: 1p; 2p; 5p; 10p; and 50p, and may choose the first strategy if he or she randomly and blindly selects the 5p say, and the second strategy if any of the other four coins is selected.

The value of any game is the expected pay-off when both players choose their optimal strategies. In the case of a two-by-two matrix, however, the value of the game is the same even if only one player uses an optimal mixed strategy. Therefore, the value of the game depicted in Example 5.3 is got by substituting the solutions for p and q back into either side of either equation:

$$\text{Value of game} = 0(p) + 25(1 - p)$$
$$= 0(0.2) + 25(0.8)$$
$$= 20$$

Note that the value of the game, using mixed strategies with predetermined probabilities, guarantees at least no worse a pay-off than other strategic combinations. From the pilots' point of view, they have guaranteed a pay-off of at least 20%, instead of the previous zero. From the cabin crews' point of view, they have guaranteed to keep the pilots' pay off to a maximum of 20%, instead of the previous 25%. The minimax mixed strategies are therefore in equilibrium. Neither faction can get a better result by using any other strategy, assuming that both opponents play optimally.

Large matrices generally

Deviating from an optimal strategy can never benefit a player, no matter what the size of the matrix of the game. In the case of matrices bigger than two-by-two, the player who deviates from the optimal strategy will be actually disadvantaged, since the value of the game is assured only if both players adopt optimal mixed strategies.

Not all games with pay-off matrices larger than two-by-two are problematic. For example, it has been shown (Shapely and Snow, 1950) that any game which can be represented by a matrix with either two rows *or* two columns (i.e. a game in which *one* of the players has specifically two strategies) can be solved in the same way as two-by-two matrices, because one of the two-by-two matrices embedded in the larger matrix is a solution of the larger matrix. Therefore, to solve the larger matrix, it is necessary only to solve each two-by-two sub-matrix and to check each solution.

Example 5.4 Student attendance

A school has a problem with student attendance in the run up to public examinations, even among students who are not candidates. Teachers must decide whether to teach on, passively supervise students studying in the (reduced) class groups or actively revise coursework already done during the year. Students must decide whether to attend school or study independently at home.

Research has shown that, if teachers teach on, year-on-year results improve by 12% if students attend, but fall by 8% if they do not. If teachers passively supervise group study, examination results improve by 2% if students study at home and are unchanged if they attend. If teachers actively revise coursework, results improve 5% if students attend the revision workshops and 1% if they do not.

Figure 5.16 shows the pay-off matrix for the game. It has no saddle point, so the players must adopt a mixed strategy. One of the columns – the first one say – can be arbitrarily deleted and the residual two-by-two matrix solved, as follows.

Let the students' first-row mixed strategy be assigned a probability p and the second-row mixed strategy a probability $1 - p$. The expected pay-offs yielded by these two strategies are equal no matter what the teachers do. Therefore:

$$0(p) + 2(1 - p) = 5(p) + 1(1 - p)$$

which yields the solutions:

Teachers

Strategy		Teach on	Passively supervise group study	Actively give revision workshops
Students	Attend lessons	12	0	5
	Do not attend lessons	−8	2	1

Figure 5.16 Pay-off matrix for attendance of students during public examination period.

$p = 1/6$ and $1 - p = 5/6$

Similarly, let the teachers' second-column mixed strategy be assigned a probability q and the third-column mixed strategy a probability $1 - q$. The expected pay-offs yielded by these two strategies against the students are equal. Therefore:

$$0(q) + 5(1 - q) = 2(q) + 1(1 - q)$$

which gives the solutions:

$q = 2/3$ and $1 - q = 1/3$

The value of this game, got by back-substituting into either side of either equation, is 5/3. If the solution to the two-by-two sub-matrix given above is the solution to the two-by-three original matrix, then the ignored strategy – the teachers' first column – will yield a worse value than 5/3 for the teachers, i.e. a value bigger than 5/3 for the students. However, this is not the case. The value against column one is:

$$12(1/6) - 8(5/6) = -28/6$$

and therefore the strategy represented by column one should *not* be ignored by the teachers.

If the second column is deleted, the residual matrix has a saddle point (whose value is 5) and so the method of mixed strategies makes no sense. However, this 'solution' can be ignored since the game does not have a saddle point and cannot be made to have one by ignoring awkward options. (The reader can check that a minus probability is always produced for p or q if such a nebulous saddle point appears in any residual two-by-two matrix.)

The search continues by deleting the third column. A method similar to the one described above produces the following solutions:

$p = 5/11$ and $1 - p = 6/11$

and

$q = 1/11$ and $1 - q = 10/11$

The value of this game is 12/11. If this solution is the solution to the original matrix, then the ignored strategy – the teachers' third column – will yield a worse value than 12/11 for the teachers, i.e. a value bigger than 12/11 for the students. And this is indeed the case. The value against column three is:

$5(5/11) + 1(6/11) = 31/11$

So a solution has been found. The strategy represented by column three (actively giving revision workshops) should be ignored by teachers. They should adopt the 'teach on' and 'passive supervision' strategies with the probabilities 1/11 and 10/11, respectively. Students should attend or not attend with the probabilities 5/11 and 6/11, respectively.

Interval and ordinal scales for pay-offs

All the pay-off matrices used so far have assumed an interval scale. For example, in the case of the pay-off matrix in Figure 5.16 (Example 5.4), it is assumed that pay-off '12' is six times more desirable than pay-off '2'. Moreover, it is assumed that the zero point on the pay-off scale is properly located, so that negative pay-offs can have meaning.

Such interval pay-off matrices can be adjusted, if need be, using linear transformations. In other words, if x represents any one pay-off matrix element and α and β are real constants, then:

$x' = \alpha x + \beta$

where x' represents a modified version of the pay-off so that all the strategic properties of the matrix remain intact, i.e. the matrix has the same relative preference values, the same optimal strategies and the same game value. Linear transformations can be used to rid a matrix of negative values or fractions. For example, the matrix on Figure 5.8

Operations manager

Strategy	20 journeys	21 journeys	28 journeys
4 drivers	2100	**2000**	2100
5 drivers	2100	2000	1875
6 drivers	1890	1800	1800

Personnel manager (row label, beside "5 drivers")

Figure 5.17   Transformation of the pay-off matrix in Figure 5.8 (each pay-off multiplied by 100).

Teachers

Strategy	Teach on	Passively supervise group study	Actively give revision workshops
Attend lessons	20	8	13
Do not attend lessons	0	10	9

Students (row label, beside the rows)

Figure 5.18   Transformation of the pay-off matrix in Figure 5.16 (each pay-off has 8 added).

(representing the game in Example 5.2) has fractions which can be removed by the linear transformation $x' = 100x$, producing the matrix in Figure 5.17.

Similarly, the matrix in Figure 5.16 (representing the game in Example 5.4) has a negative pay-off which can be removed by the linear transformation $x' = x + 8$, producing the matrix in Figure 5.18.

It should be noted, however, that while the optimal solution strategies remain the same, the value of the game has to be factored up or down depending on how the linear transformation has adjusted the pay-offs, to bring it back in line with the original zero point and scale. In the examples above, the value of the game for Figure 5.17 has to be divided by 100 and the value of the game for Figure 5.18 has to be reduced by 8.

Ordinal pay-offs on the other hand, have no regard for scale,

Hospital board

Strategy	Dismiss with retirement package	Retain & retrain
Surgeon Accept incompetency assessment	g	b
Reject incompetency assessment	vg	vb

Figure 5.19   A reconfigured matrix with ordinal pay-offs.

although they preserve the relative ranking of preferences. So pay-off '3' is less favourable than '4' and more favourable than '2', although '4' is not twice as favourable as '2'. Pay-off matrices in mixed-motive games (Chapter 6) are usually ordinal, while cooperative and zero-sum games tend to have interval scales. In theory, ordinal pay-offs can be adjusted, like interval pay-offs, by linear transformations, but in practice it makes no sense to do so.

Games with ordinal pay-offs and saddle points

Games with ordinal pay-offs can be solved easily if they have saddle points. Figure 5.19 is Figure 5.7 reconfigured as an ordinal pay-off matrix, and vb, b, g and vg represent 'very bad', 'bad', 'good' and 'very good', respectively.

It is still clear that b is a saddle point, since b is the minimum in its row and the maximum in its column. In other words,

$vb < b < g$, for all values of $vb, b, g \in \mathbb{R}$

So, it is not necessary to have exact quantitative measurements of the relative desirability of the pay-offs in a zero-sum game in order to find a solution.

Games with ordinal pay-offs, but without saddle points

Consider Figure 5.20, an ordinal reconfiguration of Figure 5.15, in which w, b and e represent the worst, bad and excellent pay-offs for the senior deputy. p and $1 - p$ are the senior deputy's mixed-strategy probabilities and q and $1 - q$ and those for the junior deputy.

Cabin crews

Strategy		Change now	Change later	Probability
Pilots	Change now	w	e	p
	Change later	b	w	1−p
		q	1−q	Assigned probabilities

Figure 5.20   A reconfigured ordinal pay-off matrix, with probabilities.

As before:

$$w(p) + b(1 - p) = e(p) + w(1 - p) \qquad \text{(i)}$$

and

$$w(q) + e(1 - q) = b(q) + w(1 - q) \qquad \text{(ii)}$$

From Equation (i):

$$p = (w - b)/(2w - b - e)$$

and

$$1 - p = (w - e)/(2w - b - e)$$

So the following ratios are equivalent

$$p:1 - p = w - b:w - e$$

Clearly, if the difference between 'worst' and 'bad' (25% in the case of Example 5.3) is smaller than the difference between 'worst' and 'excellent' (100% in the case of Example 5.3), then the pilots should assign a higher probability to 'changing now', i.e. p should be higher than $1 - p$.

From Equation (ii):

$$q = (w - e)/(2w - b - e)$$

and

$$1 - q = (w - b)/(2w - b - e)$$

So the following ratios are equivalent

$q: 1 - q = w - e : w - b$

and the cabin crews should assign a higher probability to 'changing later', which is the inverse strategy and probability of that of the pilots.

Although this ordinal game has not been completely solved, because the probabilities and the value of the game have not been determined, nevertheless the analysis has at least given both players some indication of what their optimal strategies are. This is a recurring feature of game theory as applied to more intractable problems: it does not always produce a solution, but it does provide a greater insight into the nature of the problem and the whereabouts of the solution.

6 Two-person mixed-motive games of strategy

Consider what you think is required and decide accordingly. But never give your reasons; for your judgement will probably be right, but your reasons will certainly be wrong.

Earl of Mansfield 1705–1793 'Advice to a new governor'

Whereas games of cooperation are games in which there is no conflict of interest and the pay-offs are identical for both players; and whereas zero-sum games are games in which the players' interests are totally opposed and what is good for one player is necessarily bad for the other; mixed-motive games come somewhere between the two.

In a mixed-motive game, the sum of the pay-offs differs from strategy to strategy, so they are sometimes called *variable-sum games*, although the term is not strictly accurate since cooperative games are also variable. They rarely produce pure solutions, but they are interesting for the real-life situations they represent and for providing an insight into the nature of conflict resolution.

Even the simplest mixed-motive games, represented by two-by-two matrices, have many strategically distinct types. There are 12 distinct symmetrical two-by-two mixed-motive games, of which eight have single stable Nash equilibrium points and four do not (Rapoport & Guyer, 1966). The first section of this chapter refines some familiar concepts for use in mixed-motive games and illustrates the features of the eight mixed-motive games that have stable Nash equilibrium points (Figure 6.4). The group of four games that do *not* have Nash equilibria is more interesting and is considered in detail in the second section. In fact, all two-by-two mixed-motive games without stable

Nash equilibrium points are categorised according to their similarity to one of these four archetypes, so they are of prime importance in any typology of mixed-motive games (Rapoport, 1967a; Colman, 1982). One of the four categories – that of martyrdom games – includes the famous prisoner's dilemma game which, unlike the other three, has a single Nash equilibrium, but is one which is curiously paradoxical. A proposed solution in metagame theory is discussed.

The chapter finishes with a detailed examination of the famous Cournot, von Stackelberg and Bertrand duopolies and a section on how to solve games that do not have any Nash equilibrium points, using mixed strategies.

Representing mixed-motive games and the Nash equilibrium

Mixed-motive games are represented in a slightly different way from cooperative and zero-sum games. They always use simple ordinal pay-offs, where only relative preference is indicated by the numbers in the matrix. Both players' pay-offs are displayed on the pay-off matrix, with the 'row' player coming first, by convention, in the coordinate pair.

The terms and concepts introduced in the previous chapters, such as pay-off matrices, dominance, inadmissibility, saddle or equilibrium points and mixed strategies, need to be developed further or adjusted slightly for mixed-motive games, so that the principles of approach can be rigorously described.

Firstly, the definition of the games themselves.

A *two-player mixed-motive game* is defined as a game in which:

- player 1 (row) has a finite set of strategies $S_1 = \{r_1, r_2, \ldots, r_m\}$, where No. $(S_1) = m$;
- player 2 (column) has a finite set of strategies $S_2 = \{c_1, c_2, \ldots, c_n\}$, where No. $(S_2) = n$;
- the pay-offs for the players are the utility functions u_1 and u_2 and the pay-off for player 1 of outcome (r, c) is denoted by $u_1(r, c) \in S_1 \times S_2$ (the cartesian product).

Using this new notation, the concepts of dominance and inadmissibility can be refined (see Figure 6.1). A strategy r_i of player 1 is said to *dominate* another strategy r_j of player 1 if

		Player 2	
	Strategy	c_1	c_2
Player 1	r_1	$u_1(r_1, c_1)$, $u_2(r_1, c_1)$	$u_1(r_1, c_2)$, $u_2(r_1, c_2)$
	r_2	$u_1(r_2, c_1)$, $u_2(r_2, c_1)$	$u_1(r_2, c_2)$, $u_2(r_2, c_2)$

Figure 6.1 A mixed-motive game with two players.

		Player 2	
	Strategy	c_1	c_2
Player 1	r_1	2, 2	4, 3
	r_2	3, 4	1, 1

Figure 6.2 A mixed-motive game with no dominant strategies.

$$u_1(r_i, c) \geq u_1(r_j, c), \forall\, c \in S_2$$

Strategy r_j of player 1 is now said to be *inadmissible* in that player 1 cannot choose it and at the same time claim to act rationally.

The dominance of r_i over r_j is said to be *strict* if:

$$u_1(r_i, c) > u_1(r_j, c), \forall\, c \in S_2$$

and *weak* if:

$$u_1(r_i, c) \geq u_1(r_j, c), \forall\, c \in S_2$$

In the previous chapter, the *method of iterated elimination of dominated strategies* was described as an alternative way of solving game matrices (see Figures 5.11–5.13). Unfortunately, it cannot be used to solve many mixed-motive games. The matrix represented on Figure 6.2, for example, has no dominant or dominated strategies and therefore cannot be solved using the elimination method.

Instead, such games must be solved using the concept of the Nash equilibrium (Plon, 1974). A pair of strategies $(r_N, c_N) \in S_1 \times S_2$ is said to be a *Nash equilibrium* if:

	Player 2		
Strategy	c_1	c_2	c_3
r_1	1, 0	0, 3	3, 1
r_2	0, 2	1, 1	4, 0
r_3	0, 2	3, 4	6, 2

(Player 1 labels the rows)

Figure 6.3   A Nash equilibrium.

- $u_1(r_N, c_N) \geq u_1(r, c_N), \forall \, r \in S_1$
- $u_2(r_N, c_N) \geq u_2(r_N, c), \forall \, c \in S_2$

In other words, r_N is bigger than any other r in the same column and c_N is bigger than any other c in the same row. In the example represented on Figure 6.3, three player 1 pay-offs are maximum in their columns – (**1**, 0), (**6**, 2) and (**3**, **4**) – but only the last one is simultaneously maximum in its row for player 2.

So a Nash equilibrium is a unique pair of strategies from which neither player has an incentive to deviate since, given what the other player has chosen, the Nash equilibrium is optimal. In many ways, the concept of the Nash equilibrium is a self-fulfilling prophecy.

If both players know that both know about the Nash equilibrium, then they will both want to choose their Nash equilibrium strategy. Conversely, any outcome that is not the result of a Nash equilibrium strategy will not be self-promoting and one player will always want to deviate. For example, the matrix on Figure 6.2 has two Nash equilibria – (4, 3) and (3, 4) – and it can be seen that, if either of the other pairs of strategies were chosen, there would be regret from at least one of the players.

It is worth noting that, if a game can be solved using the method of iterated elimination, then the game must have a single unique Nash equilibrium that would, of course, give the same solution. For example, the game represented on Figure 6.4 has a Nash equilibrium at (4, 4) and could easily have been solved by the principles of dominance and inadmissibility, since strategy r_1 dominates r_2 for player 1, and strategy c_1 dominates c_2 for player 2. Neither player has any incentive to deviate from these strategies r_1 and c_1.

Player 2

Strategy	c_1	c_2
r_1	4, 4	2, 3
r_2	3, 2	1, 1

Player 1

Figure 6.4   Pay-off matrix for a two-person mixed-motive game with a single Nash equilibrium point.

Unfortunately, just as not every game can be solved using iterated elimination, not every game has a unique Nash equilibrium point. The ones that have no Nash equilibrium points at all must be solved using the method of mixed strategies discussed in Chapter 5 (see Example 5.3) and the ones that have multiple or unstable equilibrium points are categorised according to their similarity to one of the following archetypes.

Mixed-motive games without single equilibrium points: archetype 1 – leadership games

All leadership games have pay-off matrices like Figure 6.5. Since the pay-offs are ordinal rather than interval, the matrix can be made to represent many games, but one example should serve to illustrate its main features.

Example 6.1 A leadership game

There are two trade unions in a factory and each has proposed its own candidate to chair the staff relations committee. Each candidate must decide whether to accept or decline the nomination. If both accept, then the matter will be decided by a potentially divisive vote, which is the worst possible outcome for all concerned. If both decline the nominations, then the divisive vote will be avoided in favour of a third agreed candidate – the second worst pay-off for both, since neither nominee benefits. If one candidate accepts the nomination and the other declines in favour of the other candidate, the accepting candidate benefits most obviously, but the other candidate retains hopes of an unopposed nomination the following year. These pay-offs are represented on Figure 6.5.

Nominee 2

Strategy	Decline nomination	Accept nomination
Nominee 1 Decline nomination	2, 2	3, 4
Accept nomination	4, 3	1, 1

Figure 6.5   Pay-off matrix for leadership games.

It can be seen from the matrix that there are no dominant or inadmissible strategies. Neither candidate can select a strategy that will yield the best pay-off no matter what the other candidate does. The minimax principle fails too because, according to it, both candidates should choose their first strategy (decline the nomination) so as to avoid the worst pay-off (1, 1). Yet, if they do this, both candidates regret it once the other's choice becomes known. Hence, the minimax strategies are not in equilibrium and the 'solution' (2, 2) is not an equilibrium point. It is unstable and both players are tempted to deviate from it, although it should be pointed out that the worst case scenario (1, 1) arises when *both* players deviate from their minimax strategies.

Despite the failure of both the elimination and the minimax approaches, there are two equilibrium points on the Figure 6.5 matrix. If nominee 1 chooses to accept the nomination, nominee 2 can do no better than decline; and if nominee 1 chooses to decline the nomination, nominee 2 can do no better than accept. So there are two equilibrium points – those with pay-offs (4, 3) and (3, 4).

Unlike zero-sum games, the value of the game is not a constant because the players do not agree about preferability and the two equilibrium points are therefore asymmetrical. There is no formal solution beyond this. Informal factors such as explicit negotiation and cultural prominence must be explored if a more definite outcome is required. For example, a younger nominee may defer in favour of an older one in companies where seniority is the prominent basis for promotion; or the two candidates may negotiate a political arrangement. Either way, it is in the interests of both players in a

College 2

Strategy	Submit preferred calendar	Submit unpreferred calendar
College 1 Submit preferred calendar	2, 2	**4, 3**
Submit unpreferred calendar	**3, 4**	1, 1

Figure 6.6   Pay-off matrix for heroic games

mixed-motive game to communicate their intentions to one another, which is the opposite paradigm to that which prevails in zero-sum games, and informal considerations are common. Games with this type of pay-off matrix are called leadership games (Rapoport, 1967a) because the player who deviates from the minimax strategy benefits both self and the other player, *but self more* and as such is 'leading' from the front.

Mixed-motive games without single equilibrium points: archetype 2 – heroic games

All heroic games have pay-off matrices like Figure 6.6. Again, an example should serve to illustrate the main features.

Example 6.2 An heroic game

Two colleges in the same conurbation are required, as far as possible, to coordinate their closures so that school buses do not have to run unnecessarily, and they must submit their proposed calendars to the local education authority by a certain date. End of term opening and closing dates are relatively uncontentious, but a major disagreement has arisen over mid-term closures.

The worst case scenario is that both colleges submit their less preferred options. If both submit their preferred options, then the outcome is not as bad, but far from ideal, since the local authority is bound to arrive at some partially unsatisfactory compromise. Much better if only one college elects to submit its preferred calendar. It maximises its own pay-off of course, but the pay-off for the other college reflects its hope of reversing the arrangement next year. The ordinal pay-offs are displayed on Figure 6.6.

As was the case with the leadership game described in the previous example, there are no dominant or inadmissible strategies and the minimax principle, in which both colleges choose their first strategy (submit preferred calendar) so as to avoid the worst pay-off (1, 1) fails. Again, as was the case with leadership games, the minimax strategies are unstable and both players are tempted to deviate from it.

There are, nevertheless, two equilibrium points on the Figure 6.6 matrix. If college 2 chooses to submit its preferred calendar, college 1 can do no better than submit its less preferred calendar; and vice versa. So there are two equilibrium points with pay-offs (4, 3) and (3, 4). Again, like leadership games, the value of the game is not a constant because the players do not agree about preferability.

Games with this type of pay-off matrix are called *heroic* games (Rapoport, 1967a) because the player who deviates from the minimax strategy benefits both self and the other player, *but benefits the other player more* and as such is exhibiting heroic unselfish behaviour.

Like leadership games, there is no formal solution beyond this, although it is clearly in the interests of both players to communicate their intentions to one another. Informal considerations suggest that it is a good strategy to convince the other player of one's own determination! For example, if college 2 convinces college 1 that it has a school tour abroad planned which is impossible to cancel, college 1 serves *its own* interest best by acting heroically and choosing its less preferred option (Luce & Raiffa, 1989). It can also be seen from this example that the commonly held notion of 'keeping all options open' is erroneous, as many game theoreticians have pointed out. Better to adopt a 'scorched earth policy', like Napoleon's advance on Moscow, or at least convince the other player of one's intention to do so!

Mixed-motive games without single equilibrium points: archetype 3 – exploitation games

Exploitation games have pay-off matrices like Figure 6.7. The following example illustrates their common features.

Ericsson

Strategy	Issue shares later	Issue shares now
Nokia — Issue shares later	3, 3	**2, 4**
Issue shares now	**4, 2**	1, 1

Figure 6.7   Pay-off matrix for exploitation games.

Example 6.3 An exploitation game

Nokia and Ericsson, two publicly quoted Scandinavian companies in the telecommunications sector, are considering a share issue to raise funds for investment. The financial considerations are complicated by uncertainty over the US Federal Reserve's intention regarding money rates. All other things being equal, it would be better for both companies to wait until the next quarter's inflation figures are known.

The worst case scenario (financially) occurs when both companies decide to issue shares now, since they will both be undersubscribed, and the maximum pay-off for a company occurs when it issues shares and the other does not. In such circumstances, market demand would support a high issue price and the issuing company would be perceived among investors as the market leader, though the non-issuing company would also benefit from increased sector confidence. Figure 6.7 is the ordinal pay-off matrix for the game.

Once again, there are no dominant or inadmissible strategies and the minimax principle, in which both companies choose to issue later, fails. Although the minimax strategies intersect at (3, 3), they are unstable since both players are tempted to deviate from it and both regret their selections once the other's selection becomes known.

The two equilibrium points on Figure 6.7 are the asymmetric ones with pay-offs (4, 2) and (2, 4). If Nokia chooses to opt out, Ericsson can do no better than choose the opposite, since to opt out as well would result in the worst possible pay-off (1, 1). The converse is true in the case where Ericsson chooses to opt out.

Games with this type of pay-off matrix are called *exploitation* games (Rapoport, 1967a) because the player who deviates unilaterally from the 'safe' minimax strategy benefits only himself and *at the expense of the other player*. In addition, in going after the best possible pay-off, the 'deviant' risks disaster for both!

Even more than heroic games, it is imperative in games of exploitation that the player who intends to deviate from the minimax convinces the other that he is resolute in his intent. Put crudely, the most convincing player always wins exploitation games! In addition, the more games of this sort a player wins, the more likely the player is to continue winning, since the player's seriousness of intent has been amply demonstrated and the player has become more confident. Reputation – the sum of a player's historical behaviour in previous trials of the game – is everything. As Colman (1982) puts it, nothing succeeds like success in the field of brinkmanship! The more reckless, selfish and irrational players are *perceived to be*, the greater is their advantage in games of exploitation, since opposing players know that they risk disaster for everyone if they try to win. This psychological use of craziness can be seen in terrorist organisations (Corsi, 1981), political leaders and among small children, though it should be noted that although the player is *perceived* to be irrational, he or she is nevertheless acting rationally throughout with a view to winning the game. (Schelling, 1960; Howard, 1966; Brams, 1990).

Mixed-motive games without single equilibrium points: archetype 4 – martyrdom games

Martyrdom games have pay-off matrices like Figure 6.8. Its most famous prototype is the *prisoner's dilemma* game, so-called in 1950 by A.W. Tucker, who two years earlier had convinced the young John Nash to study at Princeton. It is the most famous and analysed game in game theory, and the example below is a variation on that well-known theme.

Stockbroker

Strategy	Refuse to cooperate with investigators	Cooperate with investigators
Lawyer Refuse to cooperate with investigators	3, 3	1, 4
Cooperate with investigators	4, 1	2, 2

Figure 6.8   Pay-off matrix for martyrdom (or 'prisoner's dilemma') games.

Example 6.4 A martyrdom game

A stockbroker and a company lawyer are suspected of insider trading and are held in separate offices to be questioned by investigators from the Metropolitan Police Fraud Department and the Serious Fraud Office, London. Evidence from colleagues is circumstantial and is not sufficient to convict either party unless one of them incriminates the other. Consequently, investigators offer them immunity and the bonus of being regarded by financial institutions as honest beyond reproach, if they give evidence against the other.

If both refuse to cooperate, they will both get off with a reprimand, in the absence of any evidence to impose more serious sanctions. If both cooperate, they will both be permanently suspended from trading and excluded from company directorships, but not jailed. If one incriminates the other by cooperating with the investigators, the latter will be jailed and the former will have obtained the best possible pay-off – that of having his/her reputation for honesty enhanced (see Figure 6.8).

This type of game is a genuine paradox. The minimax strategies intersect at (2, 2) and suggest that both players should choose to cooperate with the investigators. Unlike the other three prototype games above, this minimax solution does form an equilibrium point, since neither player can do better by choosing another strategy once the other player's strategy becomes known. For example, even if the stockbroker knew that the lawyer was going to cooperate, the stockbroker could not do any better by refusing to cooperate. It can also be seen that the second strategy (cooperation) for both lawyer and broker dominates. So from every point of view, there is a stable minimax solution at (2, 2).

However – and this is the paradox – this dominant solution is worse than the other strategy where both players 'agree' to do the same thing, i.e. refuse to cooperate with the investigators (3, 3)! It appears that there is a conflict between individual self-interest and collective self-interest. Furthermore, the latter strategy, where both players optimise their collective pay-offs, (3, 3), is itself unstable, since each player is tempted to deviate from it. In other words, in the event of both suspects refusing to cooperate with the investigators, each will regret doing so after it becomes apparent that the other player has also refused to cooperate! It appears that neither the individual self-interest Nash equilibrium at (2, 2) nor the collective self-interest equilibrium at (3, 3) offers an acceptable solution.

Games such as this are called *martyrdom* games (Rapoport, 1967a) because if both players deviate from the minimax strategy, they are doing so to benefit *the other as much as self.* And yet, the martyr who defects from this mutuality of martyrdom will always 'win' the game, guaranteeing a better pay-off no matter what the other does! Martyrdom games have other unique features too. Unlike leadership, heroic and exploitation games, martyrdom games do not have pairs of asymmetric equilibrium points and, unlike them too, the worst possible outcome does not occur when both players choose non-minimax solutions. In martyrdom games, both players have dominant strategies and one equilibrium point. If one player deviates from the minimax, he suffers himself (martyr) and benefits the other – the complete opposite of exploitation games. And if both players deviate from the minimax solution, the pay-off is better for both.

Contrary to what is sometimes falsely described as a condition of the game, the players may communicate with each other if they so choose (Aumann, 1989). It makes no difference. They might agree to refuse to cooperate with investigators before the game, but they will still choose selfishly to cooperate with investigators when faced with the actual decision, if acting rationally.

It has been suggested that a formal solution to the prisoner's dilemma and other martyrdom games can be found with the help of

Stockbroker

Strategy	Refuse to cooperate regardless of lawyer	Cooperate regardless of lawyer	Choose same strategy as lawyer	Choose opposite strategy to lawyer
Lawyer Refuse to cooperate with the investigators	3, 3	1, 4	3, 3	1, 4
Cooperate with the investigators	4, 1	**2, 2**	2, 2	4, 1

Figure 6.9   Pay-off matrix for the level-one martyrdom metagame.

metagame theory (Howard, 1966). *Metagame theory* is the construction of any number of higher level games based on the original game. A player is then assumed to choose from a collection of *meta-strategies*, each of which depends on what the other player chooses.

Consider the case outlined in Example 6.4 and represented by Figure 6.8. The lawyer has two pure strategies: to refuse to cooperate and to cooperate. For each of these, the stockbroker has four meta-strategies:
- to refuse to cooperate regardless of what the lawyer chooses,
- to cooperate regardless of what the lawyer chooses,
- to choose the same strategy as the lawyer is expected to choose, and
- to choose the opposite strategy to the one the lawyer is expected to choose.

This two-by-four matrix constitutes the first-level metagame and is represented on Figure 6.9. There is an equilibrium point at (row 2, column 2) with pay-off (2, 2), since if the lawyer chooses row 1, the stockbroker should choose column 2 or column 4. In addition, if the lawyer chooses row 2, the stockbroker should choose column 2 or column 3. This corresponds to the same paradox point in the original game and a higher level metagame must be constructed in order to eliminate it.

Suppose the lawyer selects a meta-strategy depending on which of the four meta-strategies the stockbroker chooses. The lawyer can choose:

- to refuse no matter which of the four columns the broker chooses,
- to refuse unless the broker chooses the fourth column,
- to refuse unless the broker chooses the third column,
- to refuse unless the broker chooses the second column,
- to refuse unless the broker chooses the first column,
- to refuse if the broker chooses first or second column,
- to refuse if the broker chooses first or third column,
- to refuse if the broker chooses second or third column,
- to refuse if the broker chooses first or fourth column,
- to refuse if the broker chooses second or fourth column,
- to refuse if the broker chooses third or fourth column,
- to cooperate unless the broker chooses the first column,
- to cooperate unless the broker chooses the second column,
- to cooperate unless the broker chooses the third column,
- to cooperate unless the broker chooses the fourth column,
- to cooperate no matter which of the four columns the broker chooses.

This sixteen-by-four matrix constitutes the second-level metagame and is displayed on Figure 6.10. This metagame has the same paradox equilibrium point (row 16, column 2), but another two equilibrium points with pay-offs (3, 3) have appeared in addition (row 7, column 3) and (row 14, column 3). They are equilibrium points because neither player has cause to regret his or her choice of strategy. The paradox equilibrium point (2, 2) is clearly not the solution to the game, since a better pay-off can be obtained for both players from either of the other two equilibrium points. Of the other two equilibrium points, row 14 dominates row 7, and so row 7 is inadmissible as a strategy for the lawyer.

So the solution is this. The lawyer should choose to refuse to cooperate only if he or she expects the stockbroker to choose the same strategy as the lawyer is expected to make – otherwise the lawyer should choose to cooperate (row 14). The stockbroker should choose the same strategy as the lawyer is expected to choose (column 3). The value of the game is 3 for each player.

In theory, there is an infinite number of metagames and their pay-off matrices get very large very quickly. Fortunately, games represented by two-by-two matrices do not require metagames beyond level two, but opinion is divided as to whether the concept of metagame is legitimate.

Strategy	Broker			
	Refuse to cooperate regardless of the lawyer	Cooperate regardless of the lawyer	Choose same strategy as the lawyer	Choose opposite strategy to the lawyer
Refuse no matter which column the broker choses	3, 3	1, 4	3, 3	1, 4
Refuse unless the broker chooses 4	3, 3	1, 4	3, 3	4, 1
Refuse unless the broker chooses 3	3, 3	1, 4	2, 2	1, 4
Refuse unless the broker chooses 2	3, 3	2, 2	3, 3	1, 4
Refuse unless the broker chooses 1	4, 1	1, 4	3, 3	1, 4
Refuse unless the broker chooses 1 or 2	3, 3	1, 4	2, 2	4, 1
Refuse unless the broker chooses 1 or 3	3, 3	2, 2	**3, 3**	4, 1
Refuse unless the broker chooses 2 or 3	4, 1	1, 4	3, 3	4, 1
Refuse unless the broker chooses 1 or 4	3, 3	2, 2	2, 2	1, 4
Refuse unless the broker chooses 2 or 4	4, 1	1, 4	2, 2	1, 4
Refuse unless the broker chooses 3 or 4	4, 1	2, 2	3, 3	1, 4
Cooperate unless the broker chooses 1	3, 3	2, 2	2, 2	4, 1
Cooperate unless the broker chooses 2	4, 1	1, 4	2, 2	4, 1
Cooperate unless the broker chooses 3	4, 1	2, 2	**3, 3**	4, 1
Cooperate unless the broker chooses 4	4, 1	2, 2	2, 2	1, 4
Cooperate no matter which column the broker choses	4, 1	**2, 2**	2, 2	4, 1

The row group is labelled **Lawyer**.

Figure 6.10   Pay-off matrix for the level-two martyrdom metagame.

Some theorists (Harris, 1969; Robinson, 1975) dispute the somewhat Jesuitical solution, while others trumpet its success (Rapoport, 1967b). Either way, the solution depends on each player being able to predict what the other player will elect to do and although this is usually impossible in real-life situations, the technique at worst sheds light on what is an interesting category of game. Mixed-motive games like this are often affected by what other players are expected to do, making it important for players to conceal their intentions or to misrepresent them deliberately; metagame theory, if it does nothing else, illuminates this deception.

What experimental evidence there is supports the theory outlined above (Axelrod, 1981, described in Chapter 9). One-off prisoner's dilemma games show the predicted predisposition to selfishness (2, 2); and the results from finitely repeated prisoner's dilemma games, although they reveal a predisposition towards unselfishness (3, 3), can also be explained by theory and by the somewhat contrived nature of the situation.

Summary of features of mixed-motive prototypes

Leadership games

- There are no dominant or inadmissible strategies.
- There is a minimax solution, but it is not stable. There is a temptation to deviate.
- There are two asymmetrical equilibrium points, which are unstable because the players do not agree on preferability. The value of the game is not constant.
- The worst case scenario comes about when both players deviate from the minimax.
- There is no formal solution.
- The player who deviates from the minimax strategy benefits both self and the other player, but self more.
- It is in the interests of both players to communicate.

Heroic games

- There are no dominant or inadmissible strategies.
- There is a minimax solution, but it is not stable. There is a temptation to deviate.
- There are two asymmetrical equilibrium points, which are unstable

because the players do not agree on preferability. The value of the game is not constant.

- The worst case scenario comes about when both players deviate from the minimax.
- There is no formal solution.
- The player who deviates from minimax strategy benefits both self and the other player, but the other player more.
- It is good strategy to convince the other player of one's own determination.
- The commonly held notion of 'keeping all options open' is erroneous.

Exploitation games

- There are no dominant or inadmissible strategies.
- There is a minimax solution, but it is not stable. There is a temptation to deviate.
- There are two asymmetrical equilibrium points, which are unstable because the players do not agree on preferability. The value of the game is not constant.
- The worst case scenario comes about when both players deviate from the minimax.
- There is no formal solution.
- The player who deviates unilaterally from the 'safe' minimax strategy benefits only self and at the expense of the other player.
- In going after the best possible pay-off, a deviant player risks disaster for everyone.
- The player who intends to deviate from the minimax must convince the other player of his resolution in that regard.
- The more games of this sort a player wins, the more likely the player is to continue winning.
- Players perceived as reckless, selfish and irrational have an advantage.

Martyrdom games

- The minimax strategies are dominant at the one and only equilibrium point, but paradoxically this pay-off is worse for both players than their inadmissible strategies.

- The value of the game is constant.
- If both players deviate from the minimax strategy, they benefit the other as much as they benefit self. If one player deviates from the minimax, he suffers himself and benefits the other player.
- A formal solution can (possibly) be found with the help of metagame theory. Games represented by two-by-two matrices do not require metagames beyond level two.
- Martyrdom games represent the clash of individual and collective rationality.

The Cournot, von Stackelberg and Bertrand duopolies: an interesting application of mixed-motive games

Oligopoly is a term used to describe the situation where a number of organisations dominate a particular market and where the competitors are interdependent. As a result of that interdependence, the behaviour of one organisation affects the profits made by other organisations in the same sector. Oligopoly comes somewhere between the extremes of monopoly and pure market, but is distinguished from both by the condition of interdependency described above. In a pure market, all firms are independent of each other because the price of any commodity is set solely by competition; and in a monopolistic situation, by definition, there is no interdependence since there is only one producer.

The paper and packaging industry, dominated by two firms, Smurfit-Stone and International Paper, is an example of a *duopoly* – an oligopoly of two organisations. Their profits (and share prices) are largely determined by whether or not the market can sustain 'linerboard' price increases, which in turn is determined by overall levels of production. Clearly, the behaviour of either company influences the well-being of both.

There are three classic duopolistic models – von Stacklberg, Cournot and Bertrand – and they attempt to explain and predict the behaviour of organisations in such circumstances. In their simplest form, they are treated as one-off games and are distinguished from each other by their market structure. In the Cournot model, organisations compete simply in terms of production levels. In the von Stackelberg model, at least one organisation pre-commits to a particular level of production and the other players respond to it. In the Bertrand model, organisations compete simply in terms of the price they charge customers.

The Cournot and Bertrand models of duopoly are examples of *static* or *simultaneous* games of complete information – ones in which players simultaneously choose courses of action and each player's pay-off structure is common knowledge across the game, like a sealed-bid auction. This does not necessarily mean that all decisions are made literally at the same time, but rather *as if* the decisions were made at the same time (Gibbons, 1992a). The von Stackelberg model of duopoly, on the other hand, is an example of a *dynamic* or *sequential* game of perfect information. It is a game in which each player knows both the pay-off structures and the history of the game thus far, like an English auction, and the game has a sequence to its order of play, since players can observe the actions of others before deciding upon their own optimal responses.

The Cournot duopoly

The Cournot duopoly, as originally conceived, describes how two manufacturers selling the same product can settle on their respective factory output levels so as to maximise their own profits (Cournot, 1838). Aggregate supply is determined and the price is set, though not in any illegal sense, so that supply just meets demand, assuming that each firm supplies the market without observing the other's level of production.

The following example illustrates the features of the Cournot and von Stackelberg duopolies.

Example 6.5 The paper and packaging sector as a Cournot and von Stackelberg duopoly

Smurfit-Stone and International Paper dominate the global paper and packaging sector, though they are of slightly different size. Smurfit-Stone produces R_1 tonnes of linerboard every year and International Paper produces R_2 tonnes. The price per tonne (P) charged to customers is a function of production output; the greater the *total* output of linerboard ($R = R_1 + R_2$), the lower the price charged. They are related linearly and negatively as:

$P(R) = A - R$, where A is some fixed constant.

If c_1 is the marginal cost of production per tonne of linerboard for Smurfit-Stone and c_2 is the marginal cost of production per tonne for International Paper, both constants for the year, how many tonnes should each firm produce in order to maximise profit? The New York Stock Exchange, of which both firms are conscientious members, stipulates that firms must set their price structures and production levels independently.

Smurfit-Stone and International Paper are not strictly in competition with each other, but are partly competing and partly cooperating in a market. Although neither firm could alone cater for the entire market, it can be assumed that each firm could supply any non-negative level of output within reason, so the duopoly can be modelled as a mixed-motive game. Each firm needs to maximise profit subject to what the market will take. Once Smurfit-Stone and International Paper have decided on their respective optimal levels of production, the market price is made, the pay-offs (profits) are effectively determined and the game is assumed to be over. (The game is assumed to be a one-off.)

The cost to Smurfit-Stone of producing R_1 tonnes is $c_1 R_1$ and the cost to International Paper of producing R_2 tonnes is $c_2 R_2$, assuming no fixed costs. Therefore, the profit functions are:

$$\Psi_1 = (A - R)R_1 - c_1 R_1$$
$$\Psi_2 = (A - R)R_2 - c_2 R_2$$

where Ψ_1 represents Smurfit-Stone's profit and Ψ_2 represents that of International Paper. (Notice that the profit for each firm depends on the output of the other firm as well as its own, since $R = R_1 + R_2$.)

Substituting for R gives:

$$\Psi_1 = (A - R_1 - R_2)R_1 - c_1 R_1$$
$$= AR_1 - R_1^2 - R_1 R_2 - c_1 R_1$$

and

$$\Psi_2 = (A - R_1 - R_2)R_2 - c_2 R_2$$
$$= AR_2 - R_2^2 - R_1 R_2 - c_2 R_2$$

The firms choose their strategies independently and simultaneously, so the concept of the Nash equilibrium offers a solution. This involves drawing each firm's *reaction function*, which is a curve that shows every optimal production level for every possible production level of the other firm.

Each firm's reaction function can be found by differentiating its profit function with respect to output, giving:

$$\frac{\delta \Psi_1}{\delta R_1} = A - 2R_1 - R_2 - c_1$$

and

$$\frac{\delta \Psi_2}{\delta R_2} = A - 2R_2 - R_1 - c_2$$

If $\dfrac{\delta \Psi_1}{\delta R_1} = 0$ and $\dfrac{\delta \Psi_2}{\delta R_2} = 0$

then

$$2R_1 + R_2 = A - c_1$$

and

$$R_1 + 2R_2 = A - c_2$$

where A, c_1 and c_2 are constants. These two equations are the reaction functions and reveal that the optimal level of production for each firm is negatively related to the expected level of supply from the other. Note also that:

$$\frac{\delta^2 \Psi_1}{\delta R_1{}^2} = -2 \text{ and } \frac{\delta^2 \Psi_2}{\delta R_2{}^2} = -2$$

which indicate local maxima.

The method of simultaneous equations,

$$4R_1 + 2R_2 = 2A - 2c_1$$
$$R_1 + 2R_2 = A - c_2$$

produces the Nash solutions

$$R_{N1} = \frac{A + c_2 - 2c_1}{3}$$

and

$$R_{N2} = \frac{A + c_1 - 2c_2}{3}$$

The total output at the Nash equilibrium is therefore:

$$R_N = R_{N2} + R_{N2}$$
$$= \frac{2A - c_1 - c_2}{3}$$

and the maximum price that can be afforded by the market is:

$$P(R) = A - R_N$$
$$= \frac{A - 2A - c_1 - c_2}{3}$$
$$= \frac{A - c_1 - c_2}{3}$$

This solution, being a Nash equilibrium, means that both firms are content operating on these parameters, since neither feels a tendency to deviate.

Figure 6.11 represents the Cournot duopoly diagrammatically – the scales assume that c_1 and c_2 are of the same order of magnitude, though not necessarily equal – and further analysis is interesting, if a little complicated.

The two reaction function lines, having negative gradients, demonstrate the fact that the optimal level of production (and hence profit) for one firm is negatively related to the levels of production of the other. The semicircles on Figure 6.11 represent a pair of the firms' *iso-profit curves*, which plot the different combinations of production levels that yield the same profit for each firm in turn. Not surprisingly, profits are greatest when each firm is the sole supplier, in which case it supplies $(A - c_1)/2$ or $(A - c_2)/2$ tonnes of linerboard to the market – the intercept value of the respective reaction functions.

The sets of iso-profit curves for Smurfit-Stone and International Paper are centred, respectively, at the Nash equilibrium coordinates $(A - 2c_1 + c_2)/3$ and $(A + c_1 - 2c_2)/3$ and these production levels represent the solution. The further away a semicircle is from its axis – from its monopolistic situation – the lower the firm's profit. At the Nash equilibrium, marked **N** on Figure 6.11, both firms are maximising profits simultaneously, so the equilibrium is unique and the tangents to

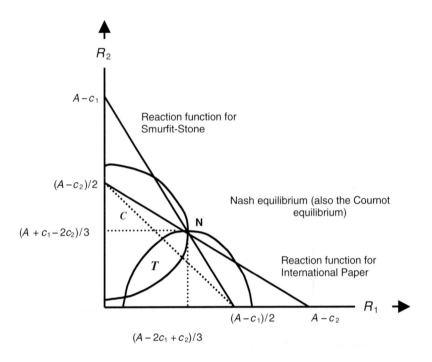

Figure 6.11   The Cournot–Nash equilibrium.

the two iso-profit curves are mutually perpendicular.

Although the concept of the Nash equilibrium has provided a solution, Cournot arrived at the same solution in a different way. He analysed how the two firms would behave if they were out of equilibrium. Figure 6.12 shows the reaction functions for Smurfit-Stone and International Paper. Say initially that Smurfit-Stone is operating a monopoly, it will produce $(A - c_1)/2$ tonnes of linerboard. If International Paper now enters the market and assumes that Smurfit-Stone will maintain that production level, it will produce at a level vertically above that point, but on its own reaction curve. This point is off the Smurfit-Stone reaction curve, so Smurfit-Stone will move its production level horizontally onto its own reaction curve. This incremental process continues, in a zigzag fashion, until the Cournot equilibrium point (C) is reached, at the intersection of the two reaction curves.

The Nash and Cournot approaches produce the same solution, but the Cournot concept is weaker because it supposes that one firm is able to react to the other firm's entry to the market, contradicting the game's assumption of 'static-ness' or simultaneity. The concept of

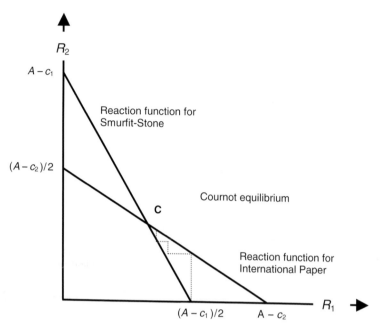

Figure 6.12   Arriving at the Cournot equilibrium.

Cournot *balance* is reasonable, but that of Cournot *imbalance* is not (Romp, 1997).

The Nash–Cournot equilibrium is not pareto-efficient. It is not the case that one player is made better off at the expense of the other. If the two firms could cooperate, they would both increase their combined profit. Diagrammatically, the Nash equilibrium is inefficient because the iso-profit curves are not tangential there, which in turn means that there are other production combinations that weakly dominate the Nash combination, i.e. one firm is better off and the other is no worse off. The combinations for which the iso-profit curves are tangential constitute the area denoted by T on Figure 6.11, which is bounded by the two iso-profit curves that intersect at the Nash equilibrium. Inside T, both firms are better off (strict dominance) and on the boundary, one firm is better off and the other is no worse off (weak dominance).

Figure 6.11 also shows the *contract line, C,* which represents all the points where the outcomes are pareto-efficient. This line therefore represents a zero-sum (or a constant-sum) sub-game of the Cournot duopoly. If the two firms could coordinate their production levels, they would maximise joint profit by choosing strategic combinations on this line. Given that they would also choose strategies inside area T, the optimal combination would be both on C and inside T. Naturally, the particular point chosen from this infinite set would be the one that divides income in the fairest way – equally if the two firms are equally 'powerful'. However, not being a Nash equilibrium and being off the reaction function lines, this optimal mid-point of C in T would be unstable because each firm would have an incentive to deviate from it. This is analogous to Martyrdom games like the prisoner's dilemma, discussed already in this chapter, and explains why cartels, both legal and illegal, tend to be unstable – each party to the collusion has an incentive to deviate unilaterally.

The von Stackelberg duopoly

In the von Stackelberg (1934) model, at least one organisation pre-commits to a particular level of production and the other responds to it. Let us assume, for the purposes of this example, that the pre-committing firm is Smurfit-Stone (which becomes the market leader) and the responding firm is International Paper. Unlike the Cournot duopoly model, the von Stackelberg model is a dynamic game, where International Paper can observer the actions of Smurfit-Stone before deciding upon its optimal response. Unlike static (or simultaneous) games, dynamic (or sequential) games carry the tactical possibility of giving false information and the need to conceal one's true intentions from the other player. If either firm believes the false production levels of the other, no matter how unlikely, the game will have multiple Nash equilibria. For example, International Paper may threaten to flood the market with linerboard in the hope that Smurfit-Stone will reduce its production to zero in response – which it will if it believes the threat – and thereby produce a Nash equilibrium. And yet, such a threat is illogical, since it would not be in either player's interests to carry it through. To exclude such idle production threats, the von Stackelberg model imposes the condition that the predicted outcome of the game must be *sub-game perfect* – that the predicted solution to the game must be a Nash equilibrium in every sub-game.

The method of backward induction may be applied to this von Stackelberg game, starting with International Paper's output response decision, which is its attempt to maximise its own profit, Ψ_2, given by:

$$\Psi_2 = (A - R)R_2 - c_2R_2$$

$$= (A - R_1 - R_2)R_2 - c_2R_2$$
$$= AR_2 - R_2^2 - R_1R_2 - c_2R_2$$

Differentiating with respect to R_2 and setting equal to zero for a maximum, gives:

$$\frac{\delta \Psi_2}{\delta R_2} = A - 2R_2 - R_1 - c_2$$

then

$$R_1 + 2R_2 = A - c_2 \tag{1}$$

This is International Paper's reaction function and to Smurfit-Stone, the only believable threat about production that International Paper can make will be on this function line.

Continuing the method of backward induction. Smurfit-Stone knows that the eventual outcome must be on International Paper's reaction function line and so it must attempt to maximise its own profit, Ψ_1, subject to that constraint:

$$\Psi_1 = (A - R)R_1 - c_1R_1$$
$$= (A - R_1 - R_2)R_1 - c_1R_1$$
$$= AR_1 - R_1^2 - R_1R_2 - c_1R_1$$

Substituting for R_2 from equation (1) gives:

$$\Psi_1 = AR_1 - R_1^2 - R_1[(A - c_2 - R_1)/2] - c_1R_1$$

which differentiates with respect to R_1 as:

$$\frac{\delta \Psi_1}{\delta R_1} = A/2 - R_1 - c_1 + c_2/2$$

Equating this to zero gives the von Stackelberg–Nash equilibrium level of production of linerboard for Smurfit-Stone:

$$R_1 = (A - 2c_1 + c_2)/2 \tag{2}$$

Substituting (2) into (1) gives International Paper's optimal production:

$$R_2 = (A + 2c_1 - 3c_2)/4 \tag{3}$$

Looking at Equations (2) and (3), it can be seen that, if the marginal cost of production for both firms is the same (equal to c say), R_2 will be

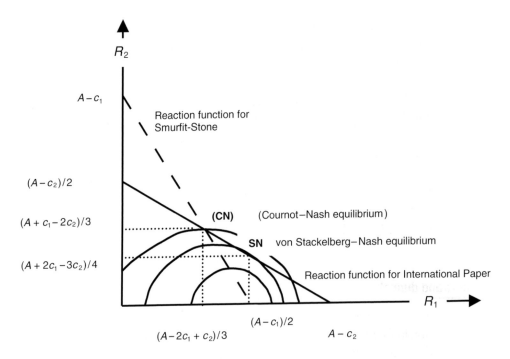

R_2

$A - c_1$

Reaction function for
Smurfit-Stone

$(A - c_2)/2$

$(A + c_1 - 2c_2)/3$

(CN)   (Cournot–Nash equilibrium)

SN   von Stackelberg–Nash equilibrium

$(A + 2c_1 - 3c_2)/4$

Reaction function for International Paper

R_1

$(A - c_1)/2$

$(A - 2c_1 + c_2)/3$

$A - c_2$

Figure 6.13   The von Stackelberg–Nash equilibrium

half of R_1 and total production of linerboard will be given by the
equation:

$$R = 3(A - c)/4 \tag{4}$$

Given that Smurfit-Stone knows that International Paper is managed
rationally and therefore will produce according to its own reaction
function, Smurfit-Stone will maximise profits where its iso-profit curve
is tangential to International Paper's reaction function (see Figure
6.13).

Smurfit-Stone would, of course, ideally like to have a monopoly on
linerboard production. On Figure 6.13, this is the point where the
Smurfit-Stone reaction function crosses the R_1 axis and has the value
$(A - c_1)/2$ tonnes. However, if International Paper's output is on its
own reaction line, the lowest iso-profit curve Smurfit-Stone can reach
is the one through the von Stackelberg–Nash equilibrium point,
marked **SN** on Figure 6.13. Effectively, at the von Stackelberg–Nash
equilibrium point, Smurfit-Stone is producing a monopoly-level out-

put of linerboard, but is not making monopoly-level profits because International Paper's non-zero production level pushes down the market price.

The Cournot–Nash equilibrium point is also shown on Figure 6.13, marked **CN**, so that the reader can see that the von Stackelberg–Nash equilibrium point means higher production and more profit for the pre-committing firm and less for the responding firm. The responding firm is actually worse off knowing what the market leader is doing and, conversely, the pre-committing firm has made itself better off by pre-committing to a certain level of production. As Romp (1997) rightly states, the von Stackelberg duopoly model is one in which the firm with the first move has the advantage.

The Bertrand duopoly

The strategic variable for firms in both the Cournot and the von Stackelberg duopolies is the level of production (R). In the Bertrand duopoly (1883), the strategic variable is the price charged in the marketplace (P). The firms simultaneously decide their pricing structures and market forces then decide how much product is absorbed. Like the Cournot duopoly, the Bertrand duopoly is a static game, but one in which the two firms compete in terms of the price they charge customers, rather than production levels.

Consider the following example.

Example 6.6 The UK supermarket sector as a Bertrand duopoly

Sainsbury and Tesco dominate the UK food supermarket sector. Competition is so fierce and profit margins so thin that it has been termed a 'price war' in the financial press. Suppose Sainsbury decides to sell a quantity R_1 of some product at a price P_1 and Tesco decides to sell a quantity R_2 of the same or some other product at a price P_2. Let Ψ_1 represents Sainsbury's profit and Ψ_2 represents that of Tesco. How would the two supermarket chains set their prices so as to maximise profits in a stable market?

In the Bertrand duopoly model, stability depends on whether or not the products sold by the competing firms are identical. Consider firstly the case where the product lines are indistinguishable. If the food products are identical, customers will only buy from the supermarket that offers the lowest price. Say, for the purposes of this example, that Tesco initially offers *lower prices and makes higher than normal profits.* It gains a monopoly, although Sainsbury is eventually forced to challenge it by undercutting prices in an attempt to win some market share for itself. However, if Tesco initially *offers lower prices and makes lower than normal profits* or none at all, then it must raise its prices to normal profit levels or go out of business. So, either way, it is clear that charging different prices never results in a Nash equilibrium for competing firms in a Bertrand duopoly.

If the food products are identical and both supermarkets *charge the same prices, and if each supermarket is making higher or lower than normal profits*, then each will have an incentive to deviate. One will slightly undercut the other to increase market share if it is making higher than normal profits; and it will slightly overcharge the other to increase profit margins if it is making lower than normal profits.

So the only Nash equilibrium is where both firms *charge the same prices and make normal profits.* The situation where as few as two firms make a competitive outcome without any collusion to increase profits above the normal, is known as the *Bertrand paradox.*

One way to overcome the Bertrand paradox is to have firms sell distinguishable products. If product lines are distinguishable, Tesco and Sainsbury face a negative demand curve and their interdependency is not as strong as when they sold identical product lines. If Sainsbury decides to sell at a price $P_1 > 0$ and Tesco decides to sell at a price $P_2 > 0$, then the Bertrand duopoly model assumes that customers will demand quantities:

$$R_1 = A - P_1 + BP_2$$

and

$$R_2 = A - P_2 + BP_1$$

from each of the two supermarkets, respectively; where A is a constant as in the previous duopoly models and B is a constant that reflects the extent to which Sainsbury's products are substitutes for Tesco's and vice versa. These two equations, called the *demand functions* for the two firms, are somewhat unrealistic, however, because demand for one supermarket's product is positive even when it charges an arbitrarily high price, provided the other supermarket charges a high enough price (Gibbons, 1992a). As will be shown below, this only makes sense if:

$$B < 2$$

The profit functions for the supermarkets are:

$$\Psi_1 = P_1 R_1 - c_1 R_1$$
$$\Psi_2 = P_2 R_2 - c_2 R_2$$

Substituting for R_1 and R_2 gives:

$$\Psi_1 = (A - P_1 + BP_2)P_1 - c_1(A - P_1 + BP_2)$$
$$\quad = AP_1 - P_1^2 + BP_1 P_2 - c_1 A + c_1 P_1 - c_1 BP_2$$

and

$$\Psi_2 = (A - P_2 + BP_1)P_2 - c_2(A - P_2 + BP_1)$$
$$\quad = AP_2 - P_2^2 + BP_1 P_2 - c_2 A + c_2 P_2 - c_2 BP_1$$

Each supermarket's reaction function can now be found by differentiating its respective profit function with respect to price:

$$\frac{\delta \Psi_1}{\delta P_1} = A - 2P_1 + BP_2 + c_1$$

and

$$\frac{\delta \Psi_2}{\delta P_2} = A - 2P_2 + BP_1 + c_2$$

If $\dfrac{\delta \Psi_1}{\delta P_1} = 0$ and $\dfrac{\delta \Psi_2}{\delta R_2} = 0$

then

$$P_1 = (A + BP_2 + c_1)/2$$
$$P_2 = (A + BP_1 + c_2)/2$$

And since

$$\frac{\delta^2 \Psi_1}{\delta P_1} = -2 \text{ and } \frac{\delta^2 \Psi_2}{\delta P_2} = -2$$

local maxima are indicated (see Figure 6.14).

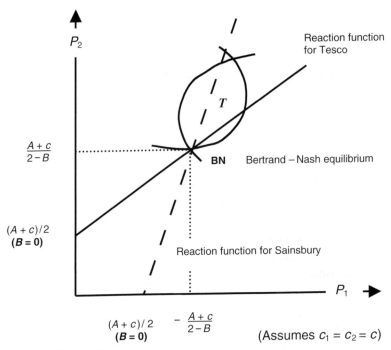

Figure 6.14 The Bertrand–Nash equilibrium.

The method of simultaneous equations,

$$2P_1 - BP_2 = A + c_1$$
$$- BP_1 + 2P_2 = A + c_2$$

produces the Bertrand–Nash equilibrium, which has solutions:

$$P_1 = \frac{A(B + 2) + 2c_1 + Bc_1}{4 - B^2}$$

and

$$P_2 = \frac{A(B + 2) + Bc_1 + 2c_2}{4 - B^2}$$

If $c_1 = c_2$, these two solutions reduce to:

$$P_1 = P_2 = (A + c)/(2 - B)$$

Note that since the price charged to customers cannot be negative, $B < 2$.

The reaction curves for the Bertrand duopoly have positive gradients, unlike those for the Cournot and von Stackelberg models. They are positively related and are said to *complement* each other *strategically*. In the case of the Cournot and von Stackelberg duopolies, the reaction functions have negative gradients. One firm's output causes the other firm to decrease its output. In such cases, the reaction functions are said to *substitute* for each other *strategically*.

To maximise their profits and to arrive at the Bertrand–Nash equilibrium, both supermarket firms must be on their reaction function lines (marked **BN** on Figure 6.14). As with the previous duopoly models, the Nash equilibrium point is not pareto-efficient, since both Sainsbury and Tesco could make higher profits if they set higher prices. This set of possibilities is shown marked *T* on Figure 6.14, but since each firm has an incentive to deviate from these arrangements, they do not offer a more likely solution than the Bertrand-Nash equilibrium.

Pareto-inefficiency is a feature of all three duopoly models. If the competitors collude they can increase profits, but since this requires (at best) an agreement that is difficult to enforce given the incentives to deviate from it, and (at worst) an illegal cartel, such 'solutions' are not realisable in practice.

Solving games without Nash equilibrium points using mixed strategies

Unfortunately, not every mixed-motive game has a Nash equilibrium, though some can nevertheless be solved fairly easily. Consider the matrix on Figure 6.15.

Clearly, there is no Nash equilibrium for this game. If player 1 chooses r_1, player 2 will choose c_1. However, if player 1 thought that player 2 was going to choose c_1, he or she would have chosen r_2, in which case player 2 would select c_2; in which case, player 1 would revert to r_1; and so on, ad nauseam. All that can be concluded from this terrible circularity is that if either side reveals its intent, it will guarantee a bad pay-off. Each player should keep the other guessing and the best way to do this is for both players to randomise their strategic selections. Random strategies thus selected – mixed strategies – have already been considered for the simple case of two-person zero-sum games, where

Player 2

Strategy	c_1	c_2
r_1	1, 4	3, 0
r_2	2, 1	1, 2

Player 1

Figure 6.15 A two-person mixed-motive game with no Nash equilibrium point.

Player 2

Strategy	c_1	c_2	....	c_n
r_1	$u_1(r_1, c_1), u_2(r_1, c_1)$	$u_1(r_1, c_2), u_2(r_1, c_2)$	....	$u_1(r_1, c_3), u_2(r_1, c_3)$
r_2	$u_1(r_2, c_1), u_2(r_2, c_1)$	$u_1(r_2, c_2), u_2(r_2, c_2)$	....	$u_1(r_2, c_3), u_2(r_2, c_3)$
⋮	⋮	⋮	⋮	⋮
r_m	$u_1(r_m, c_1), u_2(r_m, c_1)$	$u_1(r_m, c_2), u_2(r_m, c_2)$	....	$u_1(r_m, c_n), u_2(r_m, c_n)$

Player 1

Figure 6.16 The general matrix for mixed strategies in mixed-motive games.

the same pay-off matrix represents both players (Example 5.3). The general case for mixed-motive games must now be considered.

Suppose player 1 has m strategies

$$S_1 = \{r_1, r_2, \ldots, r_m\}$$

and player 2 has n strategies

$$S_2 = \{c_1, c_2, \ldots, c_n\}$$

and $u_1(r_i, c_j)$ represents the pay-off to player 1 when player 1 chooses strategy r_i and player 2 chooses strategy c_j, then the game can be represented by the $m \times n$ matrix shown on Figure 6.16.

An abbreviated version of the matrix is shown on Figure 6.17, where U_{ij} is the utility pay-off function for player 1 for strategies r_i and c_j; and V_{ij} is the utility pay-off function for player 2 for strategies r_i and c_j.

A re-definition of the Nash equilibrium can now be made for such a

	Player 2			
Strategy	c_1	c_2	....	c_n
r_1	U_{11}, V_{11}	U_{12}, V_{12}	....	U_{1n}, V_{1n}
r_2	U_{21}, V_{21}	U_{22}, V_{22}	....	U_{2n}, V_{2n}
⋮	⋮	⋮	⋮	⋮
r_m	U_{m1}, V_{m1}	U_{m1}, V_{m1}	....	U_{mn}, V_{mn}

(Player 1 labels the rows)

Figure 6.17 The abbreviated general matrix for mixed strategies in mixed-motive games.

matrix. It is a pair of strategies (r_i, c_j) such that:

- U_{ij} is maximum in its column c_j, and
- V_{ij} is maximum in its row r_i.

A mixed strategy for player 1 is a selection of probabilities p_i such that $0 \le p_i \le 1$ and

$$\Sigma p_i = 1, \text{ for } i = 1 \text{ to } m$$

A mixed strategy for player 2 is a selection of probabilities q_j such that $0 \le q_j \le 1$ and

$$\Sigma q_j = 1, \text{ for } j = 1 \text{ to } n$$

A mixed strategy becomes *pure* if p_i (or q_j) is 1 and the probabilities assigned to every other strategy are zero.

If player 1 and player 2 choose their strategies according to their mixed strategies (p and q, respectively), each has no way of knowing the other player's strategy, though the question remains, of course, as to how these mixed strategies and resulting pay-offs are calculated.

If player 2 chooses strategy c_j, then player 1 has a pay-off:

$$\Sigma p_i u_{ij}, \text{ for } i = 1 \text{ to } m$$

However, player 2 is selecting strategy c_j with a probability q_j, so the cumulative pay-off for player 1 is:

$$\Psi_1 = \Sigma\Sigma p_i q_j u_{ij}, \text{ for } i = 1 \text{ to } m \text{ and for } j = 1 \text{ to } n$$

and for player 2:

$\Psi_2 = \Sigma\Sigma p_i q_j v_{ij}$, for $i = 1$ to m and for $j = 1$ to n

The form of the game has now been changed to a game of mixed strategies and although the original game in strategic form did not have a Nash equilibrium, the game in its new form does! In fact, every game has a Nash equilibrium in mixed strategies (Nash, 1951), and pure strategies, when they exist, are just special cases in which the probabilities of all the players' strategies are zero, except for one, which is unity. Of course, every Nash equilibrium in pure strategies is also a Nash equilibrium of the game in mixed strategies.

Mixed strategies and the Nash equilibrium pay-off can be calculated from the partial derivative equations:

$$\frac{\delta \Psi_1}{\delta p_i} = 0$$

and

$$\frac{\delta \Psi_2}{\delta p_i} = 0$$

as the following example illustrates.

Example 6.7 Mutual societies and life companies changing status: a case study

In 2000, a group of policyholders of Scottish insurance giant Standard Life campaigned for it to convert to a public company and pay windfalls to each of its 2.3 million member policyholders, averaging £2500 apiece. In June of that year, the company announced that only 46% of members had voted for demutualisation, far fewer than the 75% needed to secure victory. However, a group of dissatisfied policyholders continued their campaign on the basis that the company directors were overly conservative in the value they placed on the business (£12 billion) and hence on the potential pay-offs for members.

Some members favoured demutualisation, some wished to remain a mutual society and others remained uncommitted. The concerns of those uncommitted policyholders centred largely on whether or not investment and financial services would continue to be customer-focused. Independent research carried out on behalf of one of the action groups suggested that each faction's *ordinal* pay-offs, in terms of winning over the uncommitted, were as represented on Figure 6.17.

If both factions (the pro-mutual and the pro-change) offered a community-focused bias, the pro-mutual lobby would do well at the expense of the other, since community-focus was already the strength of the status quo, although the pro-change lobby would gain some small measure of credibility (1, 4). If both factions suggested a criterion-based focus for future business, the pro-mutual faction would just about prevail (1, 2). However, if the pro-mutual lobby offered a criterion-based focus, and the pro-change lobby did not, the latter would fare better, since it would totally undermine the argument for mutuality (3, 0). And if the pro-mutual group offered a continuation of community-focused service and the pro-change group offered a change to criterion-based service, the vote would probably go the way of change (2, 1).

As things turned out, the action failed and Standard Life remains a mutual society to this day, but what strategy should each side have adopted, if they had accepted this analysis?

The game represented by Figure 6.18 has no Nash equilibrium in pure strategies, but it does in mixed strategies and so can be solved.

Let the probabilities p_1, p_2, q_1 and q_2 be as indicated, with:

$p_2 = 1 - p_1$ and $q_2 = 1 - q_1$

If Ψ_1 represents the expected pay-off functions for the pro-demutualisation (pro-change) lobby and Ψ_2 represents the expected pay-off functions for the pro-mutual lobby, then:

$$\begin{aligned}\Psi_1 &= p_1q_1 1 + p_1q_2 3 + p_2q_1 2 + p_2q_2 1 \\ &= p_1q_1 + 3p_1(1 - q_1) + 2(1 - p_1)q_1 + (1 - p_1)(1 - q_1) \\ &= -3p_1q_1 + 2p_1 + q_1 + 1\end{aligned}$$

and

$$\begin{aligned}\Psi_2 &= p_1q_1 4 + p_1q_2 0 + p_2q_1 1 + p_2q_2 2 \\ &= 4p_1q_1 + (1 - p_1)q_1 + (1 - p_1)(1 - q_1)2 \\ &= 5p_1q_1 - 2p_1 - q_1 + 2\end{aligned}$$

So,

$$\frac{\delta\Psi_1}{\delta p_1} = -3q_1 + 2 = 0$$

and

$$\frac{\delta\Psi_2}{\delta q_2} = 5p_1 - 1 = 0$$

		Pro-mutual lobby		
Strategy		Community-focused business	Criterion-based business	
Pro-change lobby	Community-focused business	1, 4	3, 0	p_1
	Criterion-based business	2, 1	1, 2	$p_2 = 1-p_1$
		q_1	$q_2 = 1-q_1$	Assigned probabilities

Figure 6.18   Pay-off matrix for a mutual society changing status.

which assigns the following probabilities to the strategies:

$p_1 = 1/5$; $p_2 = 4/5$; $q_1 = 2/3$; and $q_1 = 1/3$

and the pay-off value of the game for each player, back substituting these four values, is:

$\Psi_1 = 5/3$
$\Psi_2 = 8/5$

Therefore, the pro-change lobby should have adopted the 'community-focused business' strategy with a probability of 1/5 and the 'criterion-based business' strategy the rest of the time. The pro-mutual lobby should have adopted the 'community-focused business' strategy with a probability of 2/3 and the 'criterion-based business' strategy the rest of the time.

It may seem a strange concept, even counter intuitive, to advocate randomising strategic decisions like this. Organisational culture is one where decision makers are often inclined towards advocacy, sometimes at the expense of the game itself, so it should be understood that the randomisation of strategies is merely a subterfuge for one's intentions, since to reveal them is to lose benefit. The extent of the randomisation is then a reflection of the relative merits of each position. It may be Machiavellian, but it is not irrational!

7 Repeated games

Life is an offensive, directed against the repetitious mechanism of the universe.

A.N. Whitehead 1933 'Adventures of Ideas'

In everyday life, when people interact, they usually do so as part of a developing dynamic relationship, and when people interact with organisations, they do so on a continuous basis rather than as a series of one-off events. In such circumstances of repeated interaction, individual players learn to coordinate their strategies so as to avoid inefficient outcomes. This chapter examines how such repeated dynamic games can be analysed and how repetition affects those outcomes. It examines the important concepts of credibility, threat and sub-game perfection as applied to dynamic games.

Initially, the chapter examines infinitely repeated games where the one-off game has a unique Nash equilibrium. It is demonstrated that, provided players do not discount future returns too much, a cooperative non-collusive outcome can be sustained, but that this result collapses if the game is finitely repeated. The chapter then goes on to look at finitely repeated games where the one-off game has a unique Nash equilibrium and examines the paradox of backward induction and four proposals for avoiding it – bounded rationality, multiple Nash equilibria, uncertainty, and incompleteness of information.

Infinitely repeated games

Consider a martyrdom or prisoner's dilemma type game with cardinal, rather than ordinal, pay-offs (cf. Example 6.4; Figure 6.8).

		BUPA	
Strategy		Large subsidy for NHS	Small subsidy for NHS
GHG	Large subsidy for NHS	20, 20	40, 10
	Small subsidy for NHS	10, 40	30, 30

Figures represent profits in millions of pounds sterling.

Figure 7.1   Pay-off matrix for two private healthcare firms.

Example 7.1 Funding publicity

Two firms dominate the UK private healthcare industry: the General Healthcare Group (GHG) and British United Provident Association (BUPA) (Source: Laing & Buisson). The more the state-run National Health Service (NHS) uses private healthcare facilities to make up the shortfall in public health provision, the greater the profits made by the two firms. However, the relationship is far from simple. The private healthcare firms actually subsidise the cost of healthcare to the state by 'selling' at a discount, but their involvement and the good publicity surrounding it enhances their profits by attracting more subscribing customers.

Generally, each firm's profit depends negatively on how much the other company subsidises NHS provision. The more GHG subsidises it, the fewer recruits BUPA gets, and vice versa. If matters are simplified by categorising subsidies to the NHS as either 'large' or 'small', then the pay-offs will be as shown on Figure 7.1 (figures represent profit in millions of pounds sterling).

A comparison between Example 7.1 and Example 6.4 in the previous chapter reveals the similarity. In both cases, higher pay-offs are more desirable than lower ones (though some models of the prisoner's dilemma game focus on the penalties inflicted in each eventuality, in which case lower values indicate more preferred outcomes).

It can be seen that both firms are better off if they offer small subsidies to the NHS, (30, 30), as opposed to big subsidies, (20, 20), because if both firms offer large subsidies simultaneously, market share will be unaffected and profits will fall. Nevertheless, each firm has an incentive to increase its level of subsidy above the other (10, 40) and (40, 10).

As with the prisoner's dilemma, if this game is played only once there is a Nash equilibrium where the minimax strategies intersect, at (20, 20). Neither firm can do better by choosing another strategy once the other firm's strategy becomes known. However, this dominant solution is worse than the other strategy where both firms do the same thing, (30, 30), and the problem for competing firms is how to coordinate their strategies on the optimal outcome, (30, 30), without 'price-fixing'. In the one-off game this is not possible as there is a clear incentive to increase subsidies. However, if the interaction between BUPA and GHG is infinitely repeated, it is possible for the two firms to coordinate their actions on the pareto-efficient outcome.

Two concepts – that of adopting a punishing strategy and not discounting the future too much – help explain how and why this happens. A *punishing strategy* is one where a player selects a strategy based purely on what the other player has done, in order to punish him if he deviates from the pareto-efficient outcome. The 'shadow of the gallows' deters players from deviation and the pareto-efficient outcome can thus be maintained indefinitely. Of course, the punishment and the punisher must both have credibility, so it must be in the interests of the punisher to punish the deviant player if and when the need arises.

A punishment strategy will only be effective if it is part of the sub-game perfect Nash equilibrium for the entire game. In Example 7.1, it could be that each firm starts with small-subsidy strategies and that this arrangement is allowed to persist as long as no one deviates from the status quo. If, however, either firm adopts a large-subsidy strategy, then in that event the opposing firm guarantees to undertake large-subsidy strategies ever after.

This particular type of punishment strategy is known as a *trigger strategy*, where the actions of one player in a game cause the other player permanently to switch to another course of action. In the case of Example 7.1, it threatens an infinite punishment period if either player opts for a large-subsidy strategy. Once one firm increases its level of subsidy, the other firm guarantees to do the same thereafter, thus precluding the possibility of ever returning to the pareto-efficient outcome. The firm that first adopts the large-subsidy strategy will increase profits from £30m to £40m in the initial period, but will drop to £20m per annum thereafter. The game will reach equilibrium at (20, 20), a sub-optimal outcome for both parties.

For a trigger strategy to maintain a pareto-efficient outcome – (30, 30) in the above example – both the punishment and the 'agreement' to maintain the pareto-efficient outcome must not be ridiculous. In Example 7.1, the threat of punishment is perfectly reasonable because if one firm switches to a large-subsidy strategy, then it is rational for the other firm to also switch to a large-subsidy strategy, since that move guarantees to increase the latter's profit from £10m to £20m. The punishment strategy corresponds to the Nash equilibrium for the one-off game. This is always credible because, by definition, it is the optimal response to what is expected of the other player.

The promise to maintain the implicit agreement of small-subsidy strategies in Example 7.1 is also credible. Organisations in the for-profit sector generally seek to maximise total discounted profit, so the cooperative outcome at (30, 30) will be maintained indefinitely as long as the present value of cooperation is greater than the present value of deviating (Romp, 1997), and as long as firms do not *discount the future* too much. Since an infinitely repeated game develops over time, future pay-offs need to be discounted to some extent. Pay-offs lose value over time, so a sum of money to be received in the future should be assigned a lower value today. Conversely, a pay-off received today should be assigned a higher value in the future since it could gain interest over the intervening period.

Suppose r is the potential rate of interest, then $d = 1/(1 + r)$ is the *rate of discount*. With this rate of discount, the present value, V_{now}, of maintaining a small-subsidy strategy, $V_{now}(\text{small})$, is given by the expression:

$$V_{now}(\text{small}) = 30 + 30d + 30d^2 + \cdots$$

Therefore:

$$dV_{now}(\text{small}) = 30d + 30d^2 + 30d^3 + \cdots$$

So,

$$(1 - d)V_{now}(\text{small}) = 30$$

or

$$V_{now}(\textbf{small}) = 30/(1 - d) \tag{1}$$

The present value of deviating from this cooperative outcome and adopting a large-subsidy strategy, $V_{now}(\text{large})$, is given by:

$$V_{now}(\text{large}) = 40 + 20d + 20d^2 + \cdots$$

Therefore:

$$dV_{now}(\text{large}) = 40d + 20d^2 + 20d^3 + \cdots$$

So,

$$(1 - d)V_{now}(\text{large}) = 40 + 20d - 40d + 20d^2 - 20d^2 + \cdots$$
$$= 40(1 - d) + 20d$$

Therefore:

$$\mathbf{V_{now}(\text{large}) = 40 + 20d/(1 - d)} \tag{2}$$

As long as $V_{now}(\text{small}) \geq V_{now}(\text{large})$, the cooperative outcome will be maintained indefinitely. In other words, if

$$30/(1 - d) \geq 40 + 20d/(1 - d)$$
$$30 \geq 40 - 20d \qquad\qquad \text{(since } d < 1\text{)}$$
$$d \geq \frac{1}{2}$$

So, in an infinitely repeated version of the game described in Example 7.1, with the punishment trigger described, both healthcare firms will maintain a pareto-efficient equilibrium at (30, 30) as long as their rate of discount is greater than 1/2. If the rate of discount is less than 1/2, then each firm will deviate from the (30, 30) equilibrium. It cannot be maintained with the given punishment trigger because the future threat of punishment is not a sufficient deterrent. The players assign too great a significance to current profits at the expense of future profits, and the promise to maintain the implicit arrangement is no longer credible.

Finitely repeated games

In the previous section on infinitely repeated games, it was shown that it is possible for firms to maintain a cooperative outcome different from the Nash equilibrium for the one-off game. To do this, players must adopt appropriate punishment triggers and not discount the future beyond a certain threshold. The extent to which this result continues to hold in the context of finitely repeated games will now be considered.

Backward induction and its inherent paradox

The method of backward induction, as applied to finitely repeated games, reveals that if a one-off game has a unique Nash equilibrium, then the sub-game perfect Nash equilibrium for the entire game is this same Nash equilibrium played in every repetition of the game, no matter how many. Say, for example, a game has a unique Nash equilibrium and is played a finite number of times. To find the sub-game perfect Nash equilibrium for the game, the final iteration is examined first. This is a one-off game in itself and the predicted outcome is the unique Nash equilibrium for that single game. Both players know that in the last iteration of the game, the Nash equilibrium must be played, irrespective of what has gone before, so there can be no credible inducement or threat for a player to play anything other than the unique Nash equilibrium in the penultimate iteration. Both players know this and so the Nash equilibrium is again played. This argument can be applied to all preceding one-off iterations, so the sub-game perfect Nash equilibrium for the entire game is simply the same Nash equilibrium played in each one-off game. Therefore, a cooperative non-collusive outcome is not possible.

Consider the game described in Example 7.1, played over two consecutive years. In the second year, the predicted solution is that both firms will adopt large-subsidy strategies and make a profit of £20m each – the Nash equilibrium for the one-off game. Since the outcome for the second year is fully determined, the equilibrium for the first year must be the same, i.e. that both firms will adopt large-subsidy strategies. A similar analysis applied to any finite number of repetitions gives the same result – that the unique one-off game Nash equilibrium will be played in every iteration.

This general result is known as the *paradox of backward induction*, so called because no matter how many times a finite game is repeated, it never produces the same result as an infinitely repeated game. The relationship between infinitely and finitely repeated games is not a continuous function. There is a break in the continuum, which is counter-intuitive, since with a large number of iterations of a game, it would seem reasonable to assume that players would find some way of implicitly coordinating on the pareto-efficient outcome.

Essentially, the difference between infinitely and finitely repeated games – and the root cause of the paradox – is that in the former, the structure of the game does not change over time and there is no place from which to start the process of backward induction. A number of concepts have been developed to overcome the paradox. These include the notions of bounded rationality (see also Chapter 9), multiple Nash equilibria, uncertainty and incompleteness of information, and these are each discussed in turn below.

Avoiding the paradox of backward induction: bounded rationality

Bounded or near rationality allows people to be rational, but only within certain limits. Players are allowed to play sub-optimal strategies as long as the pay-off per iteration is within $\varepsilon \geq 0$ of their optimal strategy (Radner, 1980). An equilibrium occurs when all players play these best sub-optimal strategies and, if the number of repetitions is large enough, playing the cooperative outcome, even if it is not a sub-game perfect Nash equilibrium, can still be an equilibrium.

Consider again Example 7.1. Say both healthcare firms adopt the same punishment strategy, but for a game repeated a finite number of times, t, say. The pay-off for continuing to play according to the punishment strategy if the other firm adopts a large-subsidy strategy, assuming no discounting over time, is calculated as follows. Both GHG and BUPA are using small-subsidy strategies, so the pay-off is £30m for each firm. One firm, say BUPA, deviates from this pareto-efficient outcome and adopts a large-subsidy strategy. It increases its pay-off to £40m, but the GHG pay-off falls to £10m. The punishment strategy now kicks in and GHG changes to a large-subsidy strategy, thereby settling both pay-offs at £20m. So, the expression:

$$10 + 20(t_R - 1)$$

describes the pay-off for either firm continuing to play the punishment strategy, where t_R represents the finite number of iterations remaining in the game.

The pay-off for the firm that first deviates from the pareto-efficient

BUPA

	Large subsidy	Moderate subsidy	Small Subsidy
Large subsidy	20, 20	40, 10	0, 0
Moderate subsidy	10, 40	30, 30	0, 0
Small subsidy	0, 0	0, 0	25, 25

GHG (row player label, to the left of the matrix)

Figure 7.2   The NHS subsidy game with multiple Nash equilibria.

equilibrium, BUPA in the above scenario, is given by the expression:

$$40 + 20(t_R - 1)$$

So breaking the cooperative equilibrium yields a benefit to the deviant of £30m, or $30/t_R$ per iteration. According to the definition of bounded rationality then, the cooperative outcome is an equilibrium as long as:

$$\varepsilon > 30/t_R$$

Obviously, if t_R is very large, this condition is always satisfied, since $(30/t_R) \rightarrow 0$, and the cooperative outcome (30, 30) becomes prominent at least in the early stages of the game.

There are inherent difficulties, however, contained within the notion of bounded rationality. Friedman (1986), for example, argues that bounded rationality implies that players only calculate optimal strategies for a limited number of iterations and that therefore the game becomes shorter and the result of backward induction more likely.

Avoiding the paradox of backward induction: multiple Nash equilibria

With multiple Nash equilibria, there is no unique prediction concerning the last iteration, so players have a credible threat with which to induce other players to play the cooperative solution. Consider the following game, a variation of the one in Example 7.1, but one in which

BUPA

		Large subsidy	Moderate subsidy	Small Subsidy
GHG	Large subsidy	**40, 40**	60, 30	20, 20
	Moderate subsidy	30, 60	**55, 55**	20, 20
	Small subsidy	20, 20	20, 20	**45, 45**

Figure 7.3   The extended NHS subsidy pay-off matrix for the entire game played over two iterations.

each firm is allowed three strategies rather than two and that is played twice (see Figure 7.2).

The one-off game has two Nash equilibria, shaded in Figure 7.2, at (20, 20) and (25, 25). They are both pareto-inefficient because if players could coordinate on (30, 30), then both players would be better off. For the second iteration of the game, suppose that the two firms adopt the following punishment strategy: 'In the initial iteration, adopt a moderate subsidy strategy. In the second iteration, adopt a small subsidy strategy if the other player has also adopted a moderate subsidy strategy in the first iteration; otherwise, adopt a large subsidy strategy' (Romp, 1997).

In terms of the pay-off matrix for the entire game, this punishment strategy has the effect of increasing each pay-off by £20m, with the exception of the case where both firms adopt moderate-subsidy strategies, in which case pay-off is increased by £25m. Figure 7.3 shows the pay-off matrix for the entire game, assuming no discount of pay-offs over time.

The game now has three Nash equilibria, shaded above, at (40, 40), (55, 55) and (45, 45). Adopting moderate-subsidy strategies in the first iteration and small-subsidy strategies in the second is a sub-game perfect Nash equilibrium, and players thus avoid the paradox of backward induction.

Avoiding the paradox of backward induction: uncertainty

The paradox of backward induction can also be avoided if it is assumed that there is a fixed probability that the game will end after a given iteration, though when exactly might not be known. So, like an infinitely repeated game, the structure of the remaining finite game does not change over time and there is no point from which to start the process of backward induction. Since backward induction is only applicable to games with an end point, the paradox is avoided.

A similar analysis to that advanced already for the case of infinitely repeated games can be made, although the rate of discount, d, must be redefined. Instead of this depending only on a potential rate of interest, r, it now also depends on the probability that the game will end after any given iteration. Players now discount the future more heavily, since there is a possibility that future returns will not be received at all, so the rate of discount is defined as:

$$d = (1 - p)/(1 + r)$$

where p is the probability that the game will end after any given iteration.

Avoiding the paradox of backward induction: incomplete information

As defined already in Chapter 1, a game is said to have complete information if everyone knows everyone else's pay-off function and everyone knows everyone knows it. In contrast, incomplete information means that players are not sure what other players know or what their pay-off functions are.

In everyday life, when people interact, they are unlikely to have complete information and this lack of common knowledge complicates games and strategic selection. Consider Example 7.1 again, played once, but this time suppose GHG's involvement in the healthcare market may or may not be bound by internal financial or ethical constraints, known only to itself and not to BUPA. Clearly, the game is now one of incomplete information. Figure 7.4(a) shows the game when GHG is free of any additional constraints; and (b) shows the game when GHG is bound by some additional internal constraints.

If GHG is free of additional constraints, the pay-off matrix, shown in Figure 7.4(a), remains unchanged from that illustrated on Figure 7.1. On the other hand, if GHG is bound by some internal financial or

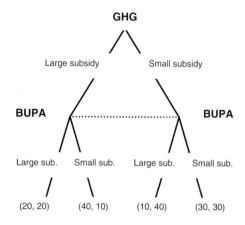

	BUPA	
Strategy	Large subsidy	Small subsidy
GHG Large subsidy	20, 20	40, 10
Small subsidy	10, 40	30, 30

(*a*)

Figure 7.4 GHG is (*a*) free of any additional constraints and (*b, overleaf*) bound by some internal constraints.

ethical constraints, the pay-off matrix becomes that shown on Figure 7.4(*b*), and GHG no longer has the strictly dominant strategy of a large-subsidy strategy. Its behaviour now depends on which type of competitor it thinks it is playing against.

It has been shown (Harsanyi, 1966; 1967) that games with incomplete information can be transformed into games of complete but imperfect information, by assuming in this case that nature determines whether GHG is 'free' or 'bound'. Hence nature determines the pay-offs for the game, according to a probability distribution, and this is assumed to be common knowledge.

This game is now one of complete but imperfect information. If nature makes GHG free of constraints with a probability p, and bound by constraints with a probability $1 - p$, the game can be represented as on Figure 7.5.

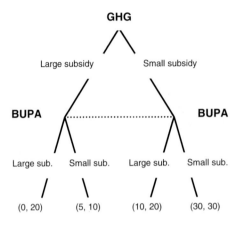

GHG

Large subsidy   Small subsidy

BUPA   **BUPA**

Large sub.   Small sub.   Large sub.   Small sub.

(0, 20)   (5, 10)   (10, 20)   (30, 30)

		BUPA	
Strategy		Large subsidy	Small subsidy
GHG	Large subsidy	0, 20	5, 10
	Small subsidy	10, 20	30, 30

(*b*)

Figure 7.4   (*cont.*)

This game can be solved using the principle of iterated strict domi-nance, which produces a unique Nash equilibrium. Row 1 dominates row 2, when GHG is free of additional constraints; row 4 dominates row 3, when GHG is bound by additional constraints. Now BUPA knows that GHG will adopt a large-subsidy strategy with probability p and a small-subsidy strategy with probability $1 - p$. Therefore, BUPA can calculate its own expected profit conditional on its own subsidy strategy. If it decides on a large-subsidy strategy, its expected profit level is:

$$20p + 20(1 - p)$$

If it decides on a small-subsidy strategy, its expected profit level is:

$$10p + 30(1 - p)$$

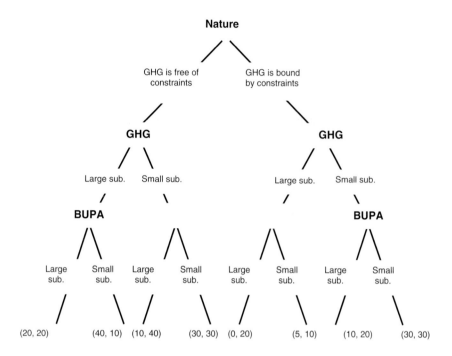

Figure 7.5   The game transformed by introducing nature.

So, BUPA will adopt a large-subsidy strategy if and only if:

$$20p + 20(1 - p) > 10p + 30(1 - p)$$

or

$$p > \frac{1}{2}$$

So if the probability of GHG being free of internal constraints is greater than 1/2, BUPA will adopt a large subsidy strategy. It is indifferent if that probability is exactly 1/2. And it will adopt a small-subsidy strategy otherwise. In this game, the healthcare firms achieve a pareto-efficient solution, (30, 30), if both adopt small subsidy strategies and $p < 1/2$.

Games of incomplete information can therefore lead to pareto-efficient outcomes, but there are complications. In dynamic games of incomplete information, players may be able to learn what other players are like by observing their past actions. This gives players the opportunity to influence the behaviour of opposing players by modifying their own actions. For example, if GHG can convince BUPA that it is bound by constraints, then BUPA will adopt a small-subsidy strategy, expecting a (30, 30) pay-off. However, GHG may actually be free of constraints, resulting in a (40, 10) pay-off. It is clearly in GHG's interest to mislead BUPA, since that increases profit at GHG by £10m. This kind of subterfuge is usual: players should cultivate a reputation for being financially or ethically constrained (in this case) so as to mislead the opposition.

Of course, players know that other players have this incentive to conceal their true intentions, a fact that should be reflected in the probabilities assigned to the game. These in turn should be determined by observation of previous behaviour and up-dated in accordance with Bayes's theorem (see Chapter 4 and Appendix B). The equilibrium concept used in such circumstances is the Bayesian sub-game perfect Nash equilibrium, which is particularly important in the case of repeated games because even small amounts of uncertainty concerning the nature of opposing players are greatly magnified by repetition. This probabilistic adjustment of the pay-offs for players often leads to a pareto-efficient outcome, so the paradox of backward induction is again overcome. (See also the centipede game in Chapter 9.)

8 Multi-person games, coalitions and power

> The management of the balance of power is a permanent undertaking, not an exertion that has a forseeable end.
>
> Henry Kissinger 1979 'The White House Years'

Multi-person games consist of three or more players and differ theoretically from single- and two-person games because they potentially involve coalitions. If the interests of the players coincide exactly, so that coalitions are unnecessary or meaningless, then the games are ones of pure coordination and reduce to the case of two-person cooperative games discussed already in Chapter 4. In such cases, the only possible coalition is the grand coalition, which involves all players acting in unison, and coordination is effected either by explicit communication or by informal expectation.

Zero-sum multi-person games, on the other hand, are radically affected by the possibility of coalition, since they introduce the potential for cooperation into a game that would otherwise not have any. These non-cooperative multi-person games use an approach which is an extension of the saddle/equilibrium point approach.

Partially cooperative and mixed-motive games come somewhere between the two extremes of purely cooperative and zero-sum games. Partially cooperative and mixed-motive games have more realistic solutions than those arising from completely non-cooperative games, although some have approaches which tend towards obscurity (von Neumann & Morgenstern, 1953).

Following a brief discussion on non-cooperative multi-person games, this chapter begins by extending some concepts and definitions to mixed-motive and partially cooperative multi-person games. Theories such as the minimal winning coalition theory and the minimum resource theory are discussed as useful predictors of coalition forming on committees. The bulk of the chapter is devoted to developing methods for analysing the distribution of power among factions on a committee. Five different indices of power are described and two in particular are developed from first principles and used in a detailed examination of power on boards of governance. Power and pay-offs for both majority and minority factions are considered, as are voting tactics and the implications for structuring committees generally.

Non-cooperative multi-person games

Decision-makers often have to choose independently from among alternative courses of action. Communication may be impossible or undesirable and there may be no prospect of forming a coalition. In some cases, coalitions may even be illegal or actively discouraged, as in the case of price-fixing cartels and share support schemes.

The formal solution to a multi-person non-cooperative game is based on its equilibrium points, which is the outcome that gives none of the players any cause for regret when the choices of the other players are revealed. The minimax theorem (von Neumann, 1928), which established that every finite strictly competitive game possesses an equilibrium point in mixed strategies, was extended by Nash in 1951 to prove that every finite multi-person game possesses at least one equilibrium point in pure or mixed strategies and that each solution corresponds to a Nash equilibrium point. In many cases, more than one solution and hence more than one Nash equilibrium point exists.

In two-person zero-sum games, different equilibrium points can be *equivalent* in that they yield the same pay-offs, and *interchangeable* insofar as any combination of strategies or Nash points can be used together. Unfortunately, these desirable features are not shared by equilibrium points even in two-person mixed-motive games, as was demonstrated in the previous chapter, because the players cannot agree on preferability. In multi-person games, these problems are compounded. There are often many non-equivalent and non-interchangeable Nash equilibrium points and there is no easy way of finding them, never mind sorting them. In fact, the outcome of a multi-person game may not be a Nash equilibrium point at all.

Mixed-motive multi-person games

A mixed-motive *multi-person game*, with n players say, is a game such that:

- each player i has a finite set of strategies S_i, $\forall\, i \in \{1, 2, \ldots, n\}$;
- each player i has a pay-off utility function, $u_i \in S_1 \times S_2 \cdots \times S_n \rightarrow \mathbb{R}$

Each player i chooses (simultaneously) a strategy $s_i \in S_i$ and receives the pay-off u_i. So in order to describe a game, the various sets of strategies $S_1, S_2 \cdots S_n$ need to be known, as do the pay-off functions $u_1, u_2, \ldots, u_n$. Each player's pay-off (u_i) is, of course, a function of all n strategies and not just the player's own.

The *Nash equilibrium for a mixed-motive multi-person game* can now be defined as the set of strategies $\{s_{N1}, s_{N2} \cdots s_{Nn}\}$ such that:

$$u_i\,(s_{N1}, s_{N2} \cdots s_{Nn}) \geq u_i\,(s_1, s_2 \cdots s_n\}, \forall\, s_i \in S_i$$

As in two-person games, it is in the interests of each player to play a Nash equilibrium strategy only if all the other players are going to do the same. Each player must know about the Nash equilibrium strategy and must know that the others know too. It must be 'accepted' by all, in which case it becomes a self-fulfilling prophecy and no player will have an incentive to deviate.

The solution $s_{N1}, s_{N2} \cdots s_{Nn}$ will be a Nash equilibrium if:

$$\frac{\delta u_i}{\delta s_i}\,(s_{N1}, s_{N2} \cdots s_{Nn}) = 0$$

and when $\delta u_i / \delta s_i = 0$ has a unique solution, then there will be one and only one Nash equilibrium for the game.

Also, each s_{Ni} will be the only stationary point of the function u_i and

$$\frac{\delta^2 u_i}{\delta s_i^2} < 0, \forall\, i$$

will indicate a local maximum.

Example 8.1 Maximising funding

The New York city Office of Management & Budget (OMB) has three sources of funding: per capita revenue from local taxes and user charges which link funding to population (u_1); additional per capita subsidies from the state of New York for disadvantaged areas (u_2); and an additional allocation from the federal government in Washington to take account of special services which the city provides, like United Nations diplomatic liaison and consular protection (u_3). The three funding formulae (pay-off functions) for the city council are:

$$u_1(a, b, c) = 36a + 5bc - a^2$$
$$u_2(a, b, c) = (a - 3b)^{1/2} + c, \text{ where } a \geq 3b$$
$$u_3(a, b, c) = 4824c + 2ab - ac^2$$

where a is the population of each of the five boroughs, b is the percentage of the population from disadvantaged areas and c is the number of man-hours spent providing additional facilities, averaged over the last three years ('expense budget').

What arrangements allow the Manager's Office to achieve maximum funding? Trial and error attempts in previous executive budgets have failed to optimise income.

It can easily be seen that

$$\frac{\delta u_1}{\delta a} = -2a + 36 \tag{1}$$

$$\frac{\delta u_2}{\delta b} = -3/2(a - 3b)^{-1/2} \tag{2}$$

$$\frac{\delta u_3}{\delta c} = 4824 - 2ac \tag{3}$$

Equating each of these partial derivatives to zero gives, from (1):

$a = 18$

Putting this value into (2) gives:

$0 = -3/2(18 - 3b)^{-1/2}$
$b = 6$

And putting this value into (3) gives:

$c = 134$

The three funding amounts, which follow from this unique solution, are therefore:

u_1 = \$4344 per capita
u_2 = \$134 per capita
u_3 = \$323 424 lump sum for special services

The second derivatives are:

$$\frac{\delta^2 u_1}{\delta a^2} = -2$$

$$\frac{\delta^2 u_2}{\delta b^2} = -9/4(a - 3b)^{-3/2}$$

$$\frac{\delta^2 u_3}{\delta c^2} = -2a$$

Clearly, all three second derivatives are always less than zero, since a, b and c are all positive numbers, so the solution is a unique Nash equilibrium that *maximises* funding income for the police force.

Partially cooperative multi-person games

Partially cooperative multi-person games are ones in which coalition-forming is allowed and sometimes even essential, but not to the extent that the games reduce to purely cooperative ones. Their study is really the study of committee-like structures, the most interesting feature of which is the way power is distributed and used by those who wield it to achieve a desired pay-off.

Partially cooperative multi-person games have associated with them the notion of a *characteristic function*, which is a rule assigning a numerical value to every possible coalition. Consider again the martyrdom game outlined in Example 6.4. Although this game (G) involves no more than two players, there are four possible coalitions: the null coalition consisting of nobody (C_0); the single coalition consisting of the lawyer only (C_1); the single coalition consisting of the stockbroker only (C_2); and the grand coalition consisting of both (C_3). This can all be represented as:

$G = \Sigma_i (C_i)$ from $i = 0$ to 3

Suppose that coalition C_i has a characteristic function (or *security level*, as it is sometimes called) denoted by $\omega\{C_i\}$, which is defined as the minimum pay-off that coalition C_i can guarantee to its member factions (von Neumann & Morgenstern, 1953). The value of the game to the null coalition is zero by definition, so:

$$\omega\{C_0\} = 0$$

The single coalition consisting solely of the lawyer can guarantee a minimum pay-off of 2 by choosing to cooperate with the investigators. So, the security level or characteristic function for the lawyer is:

$$\omega\{C_1\} = 2$$

Similarly, the single coalition consisting solely of the stockbroker can guarantee a minimum pay-off of 2, so the characteristic function for the stockbroker is:

$$\omega\{C_2\} = 2$$

Finally, if both lawyer and broker form their grand coalition and act in unison, agreeing not to cooperate with the investigators, they can guarantee a pay-off of 6:

$$\omega\{C_3\} = 6$$

It can be seen from the four characteristic functions that, if the players wish to maximise individual gain, they will form the grand coalition.

In some committee-type games with three or more players, more than one coalition may provide the maximum pay-off. The characteristic function does not in itself determine which of these winning coalitions will form, so in order to narrow the possibilities down, a concept known as the *minimal winning coalition theory* was developed by Riker in 1962. Put simply, it states that a winning coalition will seek to minimise its membership so as to avoid sharing the pay-off unnecessarily. Selfishly, the smallest winning coalition will usually form and there will seldom be an incentive to form a grand coalition. This theory may not single out any given coalition as the one destined to form, but it does eliminate some non-minimal coalitions from consideration.

A more specific concept, known as *minimum resource theory*, was developed to narrow the field of possible coalitions even further (Gamson, 1961). It proposes that factions in a coalition should and do demand a share of the pay-off commensurate with their relative voting strengths. Therefore, the coalition that will form will be the one that wins with the smallest majority.

The notion of a characteristic function – which cannot solve all multi-person games it should be said – is based on dividing the pay-off among coalition partners such that individual and collective greed are both satisfied. Martyrdom games, such as the one in Example 6.4, represent a clash of individual and collective rationality, which has to be reconciled in the way the pay-off is proportionately allocated. Such proportional payment is known as an *imputation*. Clearly, some imputations are inadmissible because they are dominated by other imputations and, when they have been eliminated, what remains is known as the *core* of the game. Each faction should receive at least what it would receive if it acted independently and the winning coalition should win the *whole pot*. In other words, the pay-off should be the same as would be the case if the coalition were a grand one.

Indices of power: measuring influence

There is a tendency to analyse power only from the perspective of how participants exercise it or how others perceive it, which is legitimate of course, but it can obfuscate the reality of having and using it. Understanding the distribution of power among players in a multi-person game is a vital undertaking, as sometimes it is the only check on the exercise of political power among the parties represented.

In cooperative multi-person majority games, coalitions are free to form and disintegrate as the agenda changes. A coalition is said to consist of *factions* – the term is not intended to indicate any belligerence – and can be defined as one or more of these factions voting together, by agreement or by chance. A winning coalition is therefore one that commands a majority of the votes and a minimal winning coalition is one that cannot suffer any defection without losing its majority.

The order of voting can sometimes be important and so it is necessary to introduce the notion of pivotal and critical factions. A faction is defined as *pivotal* to its coalition if it turns the coalition from a losing one into a winning one by virtue of *its* vote; and as *critical* if its withdrawal causes that coalition to change from a winning one to a losing one.

Underlying assumptions: sincerity, completeness and transitivity

By their very nature, coalitions often have to choose one course of action from several alternatives according to a set of formal principles, such as majority voting, designed to ensure fair outcomes. A tacit understanding underlying these principles is that voting is always *sincere* and along self-interest lines; in other words, that factions always vote for the choices they prefer, and that coalitions have not been prearranged, but come about through self-interest in order to better their pay-off.

Other axioms, like those of completeness and transitivity, also underpin the principles of cooperative action. *Completeness* refers to the assumption that a preference is real and irreversible; in other words, that factions which prefer choice X to choice Y do not also prefer choice Y to choice X. *Transitivity* assumes a consistent hierarchy of preferences; in other words, factions which prefer choice X to choice Y, and choice Y to choice Z, necessarily prefer choice X to choice Z.

There are several ways of measuring power. Two of them, the Shapley value and the Shapley–Shubik index, will now be developed using the principles outlined above. They calculate the distribution of power among factions in coalitions and their application is demonstrated in Example 8.2.

The Shapley value

The Shapley value (Shapley, 1953) rates each faction according to its a priori power. In other words, in proportion to the value added to the coalition by that faction joining it. Suppose a game, G, has n factions (not players) and some of them vote together to form a coalition C. Suppose an individual faction of C is denoted by f_i and the size of the coalition C is s, then:

$$G = \{f_1, f_2, f_3 \ldots, f_n\}; \; C = \{f_1, f_2, \ldots, f_i, \ldots, f_s\}; \; C \text{ is a subset of } G, \text{ not } \phi$$

Clearly, f_i has $s - 1$ partners, selected from $n - 1$ players. Therefore, there are

$$\frac{(n-1)!}{(s-1)!\ [(n-1)-(s-1)]!}$$

ways of re-arranging the coalition partners of i. The reciprocal of this expression is:

$$\frac{(s-1)!\ (n-s)!}{(n-1)!}$$

and represents the probability of each such selection.

Assuming that all *sizes* of coalition are equally likely, a particular size occurs with a probability of $1/n$. Therefore, the probability of any particular coalition of size s containing the individual faction i, from n factions, is given by the expression:

$$\frac{(s-1)!\ (n-s)!}{n!} \tag{1}$$

Suppose now that coalition C has a characteristic function denoted by $\omega\{C\}$, and that the characteristic function that the remaining factions have if f_i is removed from C is denoted by $\omega\{C-i\}$, then the contribution that f_i alone makes to C is:

$$\omega\{C\} - \omega\{C - i\} \tag{2}$$

The Shapley value, $\mathbb{S}(f_i)$, is now defined as the product of expressions (1) and (2), summed over s from 1 to n:

$$\mathbb{S}(f_i) = \Sigma_s \frac{(s-1)!\ (n-s)!}{n!} [\omega\{C\} - \omega\{C - i\}]$$

Regarding all sizes of coalition as equally likely may initially appear to be an unreasonable assumption in political situations, but experience suggests that all coalitions are possible and do happen in reality. Motivation by factional self-interest sees to that!

The Shapley–Shubik index

The Shapley–Shubik index is a friendlier variation of the Shapley value (Shapley & Shubik, 1954; Cowen & Fisher, 1998). Suppose that a game, G, has n factions, which form themselves into various coalitions, C, for voting purposes. Then, as before:

$G = \{f_1, f_2, f_3, \ldots, f_n\}; C = \{f_1, f_2, \ldots, f_i, \ldots, f_s\}; C$ is a subset of G, not ϕ

The Shapley–Shubik index, $\mathbb{SS}(f_i)$, is defined as:

$$\mathbb{SS}(f_i) = \frac{\Sigma_i C_i \text{ where } f_i \text{ is pivotal}}{\Sigma_i C_{i, \text{ for } i = 1 \text{ to } n}}$$

The Shapley–Shubik index is normalised, since $0 \leq \mathbb{SS}(f_i) \leq 1$, and 1 represents absolute power.

Shapley and Shubik famously used their index in an analysis of power in the United Nations Security Council. Up to 1965, there were five permanent members of the Security Council (USA, the former USSR, UK, France and China) and six non-permanent members. Analysis showed that the permanent members, who had (and still have) power of veto, controlled 98.7% of the power. In 1965, in an attempt to increase the power of the non-permanent faction, the number of non-permanent members was increased to ten, but the Shapley–Shubik analysis showed that the power of the same five permanent members had only decreased marginally, to 98%. Clearly, membership ratios are not true reflections of actual power.

The following example illustrates the Shapley value and the Shapley–Shubik index of power at work in *weighted* committees in which different factions have different voting strengths.

Example 8.2 Power and school governance in a divided society

Consider the following three archetypes of school governance boards in Northern Ireland:

Model A: *Voluntary maintained* schools, which are mostly non-selective Roman Catholic schools, typically having the following representations on their boards:
- four Roman Catholic church trustees
- two Education and Library Board representatives (ELB)
- one parent
- one teacher
- one representative from the Department of Education (DE)

Model B: *Controlled secondary* schools, which are mostly non-selective Protestant schools, typically having the following representations on their boards:
- four Protestant church trustees ('transferors')

- two Education and Library Board representatives (ELB)
- two parents
- one teacher

Model C: *Out-of-state* schools in the Republic of Ireland also educate pupils from Northern Ireland. Typically, they have boards of governors consisting of:
- three Education and Library Board representatives (ELB)
- three parents
- two majority religious representatives
- one minority religious representative
- two teachers

What real power does each faction have on each of the three types of governing body?

Irrespective of religious affiliation or constitution, schools everywhere have become more complex organisations as a result of the increased participation of stakeholders. This has manifested itself in a proliferation of committee-like structures, such as boards of governors, which mediate between society and the organisation. Representation on these committees usually reflects an imputational entitlement to power and many assumptions about the relative voting strengths of factions on such committees are frequently made. Take the case of the Model C school described above. At first sight, it appears that the voting power of the majority religious body is twice that of the minority religious body. Similarly, the ELB and parent factions are assumed to be 50% more 'powerful' than the teaching or majority religious bodies. These casual assumptions are dangerous on two counts. Firstly, they are simply wrong; and secondly, they support an illusion of participative democracy and empowerment that distracts from the need to bring about more fundamental change. The advantage of a game theoretic approach is that it can model majority voting situations, such as exist on school governing boards, so that these inherent fallacies become apparent.

An analysis of power on 'voluntary maintained' boards (Model A)

Let the five factions on the board of governors be denoted as follows:

Church nominees (four votes): C
Education and Library Board (two votes): L
Parent body (one vote): P
Teaching staff (one vote): T
Department of Education (one vote): D

For any one particular order of C, L, P, T and D, there are:

5 one-faction, single coalitions
20 two-faction coalitions
60 three-faction coalitions
120 four-faction coalitions
120 five-faction, grand coalitions

A little consideration reveals the following:

- None of the single coalitions is a winning one.
- Eight two-faction coalitions are winning ones and they all include C.
- Some 36 three-faction coalitions are winning ones and they all include C.
- All four-faction and grand coalitions are winning ones.

In summary, there are 284 winning coalitions out of a possible 325, though the three-faction, four-faction and grand coalitions require further investigation.

Three-faction coalitions

There are 36 winning three-faction coalitions. If C is first, the second voter will be pivotal; if C is second or third (12 occasions each) then C itself will be pivotal. Therefore, C is pivotal 24 times and L, P, T and D are pivotal on three occasions each.

Four-faction coalitions

There are 120 four-faction coalitions and they are all winning. If C is first in the voting, then the second faction to vote will be pivotal (six times each for L, P, T and D). If C is second, third or fourth in the voting, then C itself will be pivotal. In the case of the 24 coalitions that do not include C, the last faction will always be the pivotal one. Therefore, C will be pivotal 72 times and L, P, T and D will be pivotal on 12 occasions each.

Grand coalitions

In grand coalitions, the last faction voting will never be pivotal, even if

Table 8.1 Summary table for 'voluntary maintained' boards

	C pivotal	L pivotal	P pivotal	T pivotal	D pivotal	Totals
Single	0	0	0	0	0	0
Two-faction	4	1	1	1	1	8
Three-faction	24	3	3	3	3	36
Four-faction	72	12	12	12	12	120
Grand	72	12	12	12	12	120
Totals	172	28	28	28	28	284

Table 8.2 Shapley values for 'voluntary maintained' boards

	$\dfrac{(s-1)!(n-s)!}{n!}$	C	L	P	T	D	Total
Single	1/5	0	0	0	0	0	0
Two-faction	1/20	4	1	1	1	1	8
Three-faction	1/30	24	3	3	3	3	36
Four-faction	1/20	72	12	12	12	12	120
Grand	1/5	72	12	12	12	12	120
Shapley values		19.0	3.15	3.15	3.15	3.15	

it is C. Therefore, these cases reduce to the four-faction coalition analysis outlined already.

Table 8.1 is a summary table of the extent to which each faction is pivotal in each of the five possible coalition sizes.

The two actual power indices – the Shapley value and the Shapley–Shubik index – for each of the five participating factions can now be calculated.

The Shapley value for each faction

For the Shapley value equation in this case, $n = 5$ and $s = \{1, 2, 3, 4, 5\}$. We assume that the contribution of f_i to each successful coalition in which it is pivotal, namely $\omega\{C\} - \omega\{C - i\}$, is unity; and that the contribution of f_i to each unsuccessful coalition is zero. The results are summarised on Table 8.2.

The Shapley–Shubik index for each faction

The results are summarised on Table 8.3.

Table 8.3 Shapley–Shubik index for 'voluntary maintained' boards

	C pivotal	L pivotal	P pivotal	T pivotal	D pivotal
Number of coalitions where pivotal	172	28	28	28	28
Number of possible winning coalitions	284	284	284	284	284
Shapley–Shubik	0.61	0.099	0.099	0.099	0.099

An analysis of power on 'controlled secondary' boards (Model B)

Let the four factions on the board of governors be denoted as follows:

Church nominees (four votes): C
Education and Library Board (two votes): L
Parent body (two votes): P
Teaching staff (one vote): T

For any one particular order of C, L, P and T there are:

4 one-faction, single coalitions
12 two-faction coalitions
24 three-faction coalitions
24 four-faction, grand coalitions

- None of the single coalitions is a winning one.
- Six two-faction coalitions are winning ones – the ones that include C.
- All three-factions and grand coalitions are winning ones.

Consequently, there are 54 winning coalitions out of a possible 64.

Two-faction coalitions

Three have C voting last and pivotal and the other three have C voting first.

Three-faction coalitions

There are 24 winning three-faction coalitions. If C is first to vote, the second faction will become pivotal (twice each for L, P and T). If C is second (six times) or third (six times) in the voting, then C itself will be pivotal. In the other six coalitions without C, the last one to vote will become pivotal. Therefore, C is pivotal 12 times and L, P and T are pivotal on four occasions each.

Table 8.4 Summary table for 'controlled secondary' boards

	C pivotal	L pivotal	P pivotal	T pivotal	Totals
Single	0	0	0	0	0
Two-faction	3	1	1	1	6
Three-faction	12	4	4	4	24
Grand	12	4	4	4	24
Totals	27	9	9	9	54

Table 8.5 Shapley values for 'controlled secondary' boards

	$\dfrac{(s-1)!(n-s)!}{n!}$	C	L	P	T	Total
Single	1/4	0	0	0	0	0
Two-faction	1/12	3	1	1	1	6
Three-faction	1/12	12	4	4	4	24
Grand	1/4	12	4	4	4	24
Shapley values		4.25	1.42	1.42	1.42	

Grand coalitions

These cases reduce to the three-faction coalition analysis outlined above.

Table 8.4 summarises the extent to which each faction is pivotal in each of the five possible coalition sizes.

The two actual power measurements for each of the five participating factions can now be calculated.

The Shapley value for each faction

For the Shapley value equation in the case of 'controlled secondary' boards, $n = 4$ and $s = \{1, 2, 3, 4\}$. Again, we assume that the contribution of f_i to each coalition in which it is pivotal, namely $\omega\{C\} - \omega\{C - i\}$, is unity and that the contribution of f_i to each unsuccessful coalition is zero. The results are summarised on Table 8.5.

The Shapley–Shubik index for each faction

The results are summarised on Table 8.6.

An analysis of power on out-of-state boards (Model C)

Let the five factions on the board of governors be denoted as follows:

Table 8.6 Shapley–Shubik index for 'controlled secondary' boards

	C pivotal	L pivotal	P pivotal	T pivotal
Number coalitions where pivotal	27	9	9	9
Number of possible winning coalitions	54	54	54	54
Shapley–Shubik	0.50	0.167	0.167	0.167

> Education and Library Board (three votes): L
> Parent body (three votes): P
> Majority religious body (two votes): R
> Minority religious body (one vote): r
> Teaching staff (two votes): T

For any one particular order of L, P, R, r and T, there are:

> 5 one-faction, single coalitions
> 20 two-faction coalitions
> 60 three-faction coalitions
> 120 four-faction coalitions
> 120 five-faction, grand coalitions

- None of the single coalitions is a winning one.
- Only two of the two-faction coalitions are winning ones (LP and PL).
- The only three-faction coalitions that are not winning ones are the six variations of TrR.
- All four-faction and grand coalitions are winning ones.

Consequently, there are 296 winning coalitions out of a possible 325, but the three-faction, four-faction and grand coalitions require further investigation.

Three-faction coalitions

There are 54 winning three-faction coalitions. Twelve of these finish with voting from L; 12 with voting from P; and 10 with voting from each of R, T and r. Of these last 30, six start with PL or LP. Therefore, L and P are each pivotal in 15 three-faction coalitions; and R, T and r are each pivotal in eight.

Four-faction coalitions

There are 120 four-faction coalitions, all winning, and in one-fifth of them, L votes first. One-quarter of those 24 times, P will vote next, so P

Table 8.7 Summary table for 'out-of-state' boards

	L pivotal	P pivotal	R pivotal	T pivotal	r pivotal	Totals
Single	0	0	0	0	0	0
Two-faction	1	1	0	0	0	2
Three-faction	15	15	8	8	8	54
Four-faction	36	36	16	16	16	120
Grand	36	36	16	16	16	120
Totals	88	88	40	40	40	296

will be pivotal in these six coalitions. R, T and r (in any order) will vote first on a further 12 occasions and, half that time, P will be pivotal. In all other coalitions, the pivotal position will be third in the voting and P will be in this position on 24 occasions. In total then, P will be pivotal for 36 coalitions.

Similar analysis reveals that L will also be pivotal for 36 four-faction coalitions and R, T and r will each be pivotal for 16.

Grand coalitions

Since grand coalitions have 11 votes and the largest faction commands only three, the last faction voting can never be pivotal. Therefore, these cases reduce to the four-faction coalition analysis outlined above.

Table 8.7 is a summary table of the extent to which each faction is pivotal in each of the five possible coalition sizes.

The Shapley value and the Shapley–Shubik index for each of the five participating factions can now be calculated.

The Shapley value for each faction

For the Shapley value equation in the case of 'out-of-state boards', $n = 5$ and $s = \{1, 2, 3, 4, 5\}$. We assume that the contribution of f_i to each coalition in which it is pivotal, namely $\omega\{C\} - \omega\{C - i\}$, is unity and that the contribution of f_i to each unsuccessful coalition is zero. The results are summarised on Table 8.8.

The Shapley–Shubik index for each faction

The results are summarised on Table 8.9.

Table 8.8 Shapley values for 'out-of-state' boards

	$\dfrac{(s-1)!(n-s)!}{n!}$ L	P	R	T	r	Total
Single	1/5	0	0	0	0	0	0
Two-faction	1/20	1	1	0	0	0	2
Three-faction	1/30	15	15	8	8	8	54
Four-faction	1/20	36	36	16	16	16	120
Grand	1/5	36	36	16	16	16	120
Shapley values		9.55	9.55	4.27	4.27	4.27	

Table 8.9 Shapley–Shubik index for 'out-of-state' boards

	L pivotal	P pivotal	R pivotal	T pivotal	r pivotal
Number of coalitions where pivotal	88	88	40	40	40
Number of possible winning coalitions	296	296	296	296	296
Shapley–Shubik	0.297	0.297	0.135	0.135	0.135

Conclusions

The relative power of major and minor players

- On 'voluntary maintained' boards, the church nominees have four seats on the board. Parent, teacher and Department of Education (DE) representatives have one each, while the Education and Library Board (ELB) has two seats. However, analysis reveals that church nominees have more than six times the power of any of the other factions!

- On 'controlled secondary' boards, the church nominees have four seats on the board, and parent and ELB representatives have two each. There is one teacher seat. Analysis from both indices reveals that church nominees have three times the power of any of the other factions.

- On the sample 'out-of-state' board, the Shapley value and the Shapley–Shubik index both reveal that the power of the ELB faction and the parent body is approximately 2.2 times that of each of the other three factions. This is a truer reflection of power than the ratio of memberships: 3:2 in the case of both teachers and majority religious factions; 3:1 in the case of the minority religious body.

- The distribution of power is most balanced on 'out-of-state' boards and most skewed in favour of the majority on 'voluntary maintained' boards – twice as much in fact as the skew towards the majority on 'controlled secondary' boards.

The relative power of the minor players

- On 'voluntary maintained' boards, the minor factions all have equal power. The ELB does not have twice the strength of parents, teachers or DE, as might be assumed. This is a reflection of the fact that each of the four minor factions is equally 'useful' in forming winning coalitions.
- The minor factions all have equal power on 'controlled' boards too – a minor pleasant surprise for teachers, but a disappointment to parents and the ELB.
- On the sample 'out-of-state' board, both indices reveal that the power of the minority religious body is the same as that of the majority religious body, although first impressions would suggest that the latter was twice as powerful.
- It is interesting and perhaps significant that majority and minority religious bodies wield equal influence on 'out-of-state' boards, despite the different number of seats. It may encourage cooperation while maintaining a countenance of proportionality.

The pay-off for winning coalitions

- If the Shapley value was used to award pay-offs commensurate with contribution, as suggested by minimum resource theory (Gamson, 1961), then it would be a way of achieving a market-like outcome where a market did not exist *per se*, such as with school boards of governors. However, members of boards of governors are not rewarded in market-like terms, if at all, and the motivational pay-off for the pivotal factions can best be understood in terms of political influence and control. Experience suggests that the pay-off for a winning coalition is simply that its members are perceived to be influential and share, to a greater or lesser extent, the power and control associated with winning.

Table 8.10 Most pivotal position in the voting sequence for 'voluntary maintained' board factions

	% times pivotal in 2nd	% times pivotal in 3rd	% times pivotal in 4th
C	37	35	28
L	57	0	43
P	57	0	43
T	57	0	43
D	57	0	43

The order of voting or coalescence

- Although not all committee decisions are made on the basis of voting (and some votes are taken by secret ballot where the order is unimportant), nevertheless, open voting (or making known one's voting intentions) is a common occurence on committees. Table 8.10 reveals that minority factions on 'maintained' boards should avoid voting third! Voting second is slightly better than voting third (57% of the time the faction will be pivotal, as opposed to 43%), though it does not matter so much for the four church members.

  Voting first or last means that the faction cannot be pivotal, so there is a commensurate loss of power in so doing.
- On 'controlled' boards, Table 8.11 reveals that, even for the majority faction (the church nominees), there is no great advantage to coalescing second as opposed to third (56% as opposed to 44%), but again, factions should avoid voting first or last.
- On 'out-of-state' boards, analysis reveals that a faction is most powerfully placed when it is the third faction to make its position known. This is particularly so for the three minor factions, as Table 8.12 shows. It can be seen that, for these to be pivotal, they must coalesce third in the winning coalition. Even for the two majority factions, there is considerable advantage to voting third in the order, and second is slightly better than fourth. As always, factions should avoid voting first or last.

Minimal winning coalitions

- Coalescing with the pivotally positioned faction is the next-best thing to being pivotal oneself. If it is assumed that there is no political reward for losing, and that all factions want to share the spoils of winning, then the strategy should always be to end up on

Table 8.11 Most pivotal position in the voting sequence for 'controlled secondary' board factions

	% times pivotal in 2nd	% times pivotal in 3rd
C	56	44
L	56	44
P	56	44
T	56	44

Table 8.12 Most pivotal position in the voting sequence for 'out-of-state' board factions

	% times pivotal in 2nd	% times pivotal in 3rd	% times pivotal in 4th
L	18	68	14
P	18	68	14
R	0	100	0
T	0	100	0
r	0	100	0

the winning side. Unfortunately, this is opposed by an equal and opposite desire on the part of those who have already formed a winning coalition not to accept superfluous members. Just as there is no incentive for the last voting faction to dissent, there is no incentive for the first three or four factions to form grand coalitions, since the last faction is never 'important'. This idea is analogous to the minimal winning coalition theory referred to previously (Riker, 1962), which states that if a coalition is large enough to win it should avoid accepting additional factions, since these new members will demand to share in the pay-off without contributing essential votes to the consortium.

This idea of minimal winning coalitions forms the basis for another power index – the Deegan–Packel index – which is discussed below.

Other applications

While this discussion has concentrated on school governance, analysis of this sort can easily be applied to other competitive voting situations, both within education and without. For example, when the forerunner of the European Union was set up by the Treaty of Rome in 1958, there were five member states, of which Luxembourg was one. Luxembourg had one vote out of a total of seventeen, but it has subsequently been shown that no coalition of member states ever needed Luxembourg in order to achieve a majority. In effect, Luxembourg was a powerless bystander in terms of competitive voting, though no doubt it benefited in other ways from membership of the 'grand coalition'.

Implications for forming committees

Game theory analysis of multi-person coalitions raises additional practical implications for how committees are constituted, whether they are dissemination forums or statutory decision-making bodies.

- The numerical voting strength of a faction on a committee is not a reflection of its real voting power. This can lead to frustration, but it can also be a source of stability.
- Statutory decision-making committees should be constituted so as to reflect accurately the desired or entitled proportional representation.
- Managers need to be aware of the possibility of disproportionate voting power, particularly when setting up structures for staff involvement in decision making. Staff committees, which appear to reflect the relative sizes of different groupings within organisations for example, may be dangerously skewed.

There are other measurements of power, such as the Johnston index (Johnston, 1978), which looks at the reciprocal of the number of critical factions; the Deegan–Packel index (Deegan & Packel, 1978), which looks at the reciprocal of the number of minimal factions; and the Banzhaf index (Banzhaf, 1965), which looks at the number of coalitions for which a faction is both critical and pivotal.

The Johnston index

The Johnston index uses the reciprocal of the number of critical factions as its base.

Suppose, as before and using the same notation, that some of the n factions in the game vote together to form a winning coalition C. Suppose an individual faction of C is denoted by f_i and the size of the winning coalition C is s. Then:

$$C = \{f_1, f_2, \ldots, f_i, \ldots, f_s\}$$

Let k be the number of such winning coalitions in the game for which the defection of f_i is critical. Then:

Winning coalitions in which f_i is critical $= \{C_1, C_2 \cdots C_i \cdots C_k\}$

Let the number of critical factions in any coalition be denoted by m, where $m < s$. Then, m_1 denotes the number of critical factions in C_1; m_2 denotes the number of critical factions in C_2; m_i denotes the number of critical factions in C_i; m_k denotes the number of critical factions in C_k; and so on.

The total Johnston power is now defined as:

$$\mathbb{jp}(f_i) = 1/m_1 + 1/m_2 + \cdots + 1/m_i + \cdots + 1/m_k$$

and this is normalised to the Johnston index, $\mathbb{J}(f_i)$, as:

$$\mathbb{J}(f_i) = \frac{\mathbb{jp}(f_i)}{\Sigma_i \, \mathbb{jp}(f_i), \text{ for } i = 1 \text{ to } n}$$

Since the Johnston index is normalised, $0 \leq \mathbb{J}(f_i) \leq 1$, where 1 represents absolute power.

The Deegan–Packel index

The Deegan–Packel index uses the reciprocal of the number of minimal factions as its base. Let k be the number of minimal winning coalitions. Let the number of factions in any coalition be denoted by m, such that m_1 denotes the number of factions in C_1; m_2 denotes the number of factions in C_2; m_i denotes the number of factions in C_i; m_k denotes the number of factions in C_k; and so on. Using the same notations as before, the total Deegan–Packel power is defined as:

$$\mathbb{dp}(f_i) = 1/m_1 + 1/m_2 + \cdots + 1/m_i + \cdots + 1/m_k$$

and this is normalised to the Deegan–Packel index, $\mathbb{D}(f_i)$, as:

$$\mathbb{D}(f_i) = \frac{\mathbb{dp}(f_i)}{\Sigma_i \, \mathbb{dp}(f_i), \text{ for } i = 1 \text{ to } n}$$

Since the Deegan–Packel index is normalised, $0 \leq \mathbb{D}(f_i) \leq 1$, where 1 represents absolute power.

The Banzhaf index

The Banzhaf index looks at the number of coalitions for which a faction is both critical and pivotal. Using the same notation as before, the total Banzhaf power, $\mathbb{b}(f_i)$, is defined as the number of winning coalitions in which f_i is a pivotal and critical member. This is normalised to the Banzhaf index, $\mathbb{B}(f_i)$, as:

$$\mathbb{B}(f_i) = \frac{\mathbb{b}(f_i)}{\Sigma_i \ \mathbb{b}(f_i), \ \text{for } i = 1 \text{ to } n}$$

Since the Banzhaf index is normalised, $0 \leq \mathbb{B}(f_i) \leq 1$, where 1 represents absolute power.

Summary

Each of the five power indices has its own characteristics. Three of them – the Shapley, Shapley–Shubik and Banzhaf indices – depend on the order in which the winning coalition is formed. The Johnston index, which looks at coalitions that are winning but not minimal, may contain factions that are not critical, i.e. their defection does not cause the coalition to become a losing one. The Deegan–Packel index looks at the number of factions in minimal winning coalitions and thus regards all such factions as having equal power.

The two indices used in Example 8.2 are the most straightforward and popular, although they are limited in a minor way by the axioms and assumptions already noted. These include the assumption that factions always vote sincerely and along rational self-interest lines; that voting is open; that coalitions have not been pre-arranged; that all coalitions are equally likely to appear; and that there is a reward for being part of a winning coalition. The appropriateness of these assumptions is, of course, a matter for judgement. Each faction judges the suitability of a particular solution according to the favourableness of its outcomes and not by any innate attractiveness. Therefore, power is ultimately judged by its actual exercise, rather than by its perceived distribution; and perceptions can be mistaken, as game theoretic analysis shows. The actual exercise of authority and influence is a different matter. The constitution of powerful committees is sometimes taken as representative of something deeper happening in society generally, as notions about democratisation and empowerment are transferred to and from different organisational settings. However, as this chapter has illustrated, the perception of how power is distributed, never mind exercised, is often flattering to deceive. The reality is often disappointing.

9 A critique of game theory

How selfish soever man may be supposed, there are evidently some principles in his nature which interest him in the fortunes of others, and render their happiness necessary to him, though he deserves nothing from it except the pleasure of seeing it.

Adam Smith 1795 'The Theory of Moral Sentiments'

Although game theory has been outstandingly successful at developing a deeper understanding of how rational players make decisions under interdependent circumstances, several criticisms have been made of some of its assumptions. Some are fatuous; others are challenging. Among the former, is the criticism that players who act irrationally gain the upper hand in some games and that, therefore, the rational basis for game theory is undermined. This only needs to be stated for its absurdity to become apparent. It is the *perception* that players are unpredictable and irrational that gives them the edge in some games, not irrationality itself. In fact, they are being eminently rational in deliberately giving that impression, while attempting to win the game by the same conscious or subconscious manoeuvre.

Of the serious challenges to game theory mounted over the last few years, the three issues of rationality, indeterminacy and inconsistency are the most interesting. Being unresolved, it is fitting that the book finishes with them and if the reader is enticed to greater study as a result, their inclusion will have been profitable.

Rationality

Game theory is based on a presumption of rationality, which at first sight appears to be optimistic. At the very least, there is need for more experimental evidence to support the contention that individuals select critical strategies and make complex decisions under uncertainty, on the basis of rationality. Furthermore, in games which have no rational solution, it may even be the case that players have to resort to some kind of irrationality in order to progress.

The assumption of rationality in game theory can be partly justified on a number of different levels. Firstly, there is some evidence to suggest that a kind of natural selection is at work which inclines successive generations of decision makers towards the rational, on the basis that organisations which select sub-optimal strategies eventually shut down in the face of competition. Thus, successive generations of decisions are increasingly rational, although the extent to which this 'competitive evolution' applies to all commercial and not-for-profit sectors is unknown.

Secondly, justification can be demonstrated to hinge on which of the various definitions of rationality is selected. *Instrumental rationality*, for one, is the presumption that players always act selfishly in their own interest ('homo economicus' (von Neumann, 1928)) and that they are able to determine, at least probabilistically, the outcome of their actions and to rank them in order of preference. Thus, if a player makes a seemingly crazy choice, it is because the player bases selection on an irrational belief. Although the belief itself is irrational and not the selection, defining rationality thus, on the basis of outcome, is suspect. For one thing, it is sometimes self-defeating in that a player may achieve an optimal outcome by *not* acting selfishly, as in the case of the prisoner's dilemma game. Instrumental rationality suggests that the players in such a game should refuse to cooperate, yet they can both do better by rejecting this strategy. It seems that what is at work in these circumstances is not irrationality, but another type of rationality – *collective* rationality.

One alternative definition of rationality that is often discussed in relation to game theory is based on the work of Kant in the eighteenth century (Beck, 1969; Beck, 1988; Guyer & Wood, 1998). Kant defines rationality as behaviour in line with *categorical imperatives* or laws that prescribe a certain type of behaviour derived from reason alone. Since all individuals are endowed with the ability to reason, rationality dictates behaviours with which everyone can agree and all individuals use their ability to reason to formulate the same imperatives. Rational players should therefore behave according to laws which they would like to see made universal, by virtue of their rationality. If it is not possible for every player to select a certain strategy, then it is, by definition, irrational. Decisions based on Kant's notion of moral imperative, rather than on the concept of self-interest, can lead to different outcomes for game theoretic problems because players may still be acting rationally even though they have chosen unselfishness, simply because not all players find it possible morally to choose selfishness. So, depending on definition, it may yet be rational for players in a prisoner's dilemma game to cooperate after all.

Kantian and instrumental rationality are extreme alternatives to one another and there are many less radical definitions that lie somewhere between these two. One such is the notion of *bounded rationality* (Simon, 1997). According to this concept, individuals have limited computational ability and as a result, sometimes adopt very simple decision-making rules to achieve desired outcomes. These can be very successful and can sometimes outperform more 'rational' decision-making algorithms.

The most compelling evidence for this comes from an experiment designed and conducted by Robert Axelrod (1981). He invited game theorists to submit computer programs on how best to play a repeated (200 times) prisoner's dilemma game. The 14 entrants were randomly paired in a round-robin competition against each other (repeated five times) and each program's aggregate score against every other program was calculated.

The most successful strategy was the simplest one – the so-called 'tit-for-tat' strategy submitted by Anatole Rapaport – whose opening gambit was cooperation and whose subsequent moves just mimicked whatever the opponent had done previously. Axelrod later conducted a follow-up experiment. He made participants aware of tit-for-tat's strategy and invited participants to re-design their programs to beat it. At first, 'aggressive' programs did well at the expense of tit-for-tat, but the more often the aggressive programs played each other, the better tit-for-tat did. It won again! Commenting on the result, Rapaport noted that his strategy did not actually beat any of its opponents, but triumphed because opposing strategies designed to beat tit-for-tat reduced each other's scores by playing against each other.

Rapaport's winning strategy did have an Achilles' heel, however. It got locked into a losing strategy for both itself and its opponent whenever the opponent made random irrational errors – a doomsday scenario from which was needed another irrational error from the opponent in order to escape. To investigate further, Axelrod conducted a third run of the experiment, generating random error for tit-for-tat and its opponents. This time it was beaten by more tolerant opponents – ones which waited to see whether aggression was a mistake or a deliberate strategy.

The paradox that sometimes it is rational to act irrationally can only be resolved by altering the definition of what it means to be rational. The importance of such a definition is more than mere semantics. The success or otherwise of game theory as a model for behaviour depends on it. It may mean different things in different circumstances to different people, but it undermines or underpins the very foundations of game theory, whatever it is.

Indeterminacy

The second major criticism of game theoretic constructs is that they sometimes fail to deliver unique solutions, usually because the game has more than one equilibrium. In such cases, the optimal strategy remains undetermined and selections are usually made on the basis of what players think other players will do. Therefore, strategic selection is not necessarily rational. It may centre on prominent features of the game – focal points towards which decision making gravitates (Schelling, 1960). These salient features act like beacons for those playing the game, so that the final outcome is in equilibrium. They are usually experiential or cultural, rather than rational.

The problem of indeterminacy affects, in particular, mixed-strategy Nash equilibrium solutions because, if one player expects the other to choose a mixed strategy, then he or she has no reason to prefer a mixed strategy to a pure one. To overcome this, some writers have suggested that mixed-strategy probabilities represent what players subjectively believe other players will do, rather than what they will actually do (Aumann, 1987). This is akin to the *Harsanyi doctrine*, which states that if rational players have the same information, then they must necessarily share the same beliefs, although it is undermined in turn by the fact

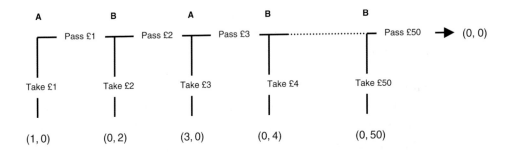

Player A pay-offs shown first

Figure 9.1 The centipede game.

that rational players with the same information do not always make the same suggestions or reach similar conclusions.

Inconsistency

The third major criticism of game theory, that of inconsistency (Binmore, 1987), concerns the technique of backward induction and the assumption of common knowledge of rationality in Bayesian sub-game perfect Nash equilibria. The criticism is best illustrated by way of an example.

The *centipede game*, so-called because of the appearance of its game tree, was developed by Rosenthal (1981) from Selten (1978), and has since been extended to include a number of variations (Megiddo, 1986; Aumann, 1988; McKelvey & Palfrey, 1992). The original basic version has two players, A and B, sitting across from each other at a table. A referee puts £1 on the table. Player A is given the choice of taking it and ending the game, or not taking it, in which case the referee adds another £1 and offers player B the same choice – take the £2 and end the game, or pass it back to the referee who will add another £1 and offer the same choice to player A again. The pot of money is allowed to grow until some pre-arranged limit is reached – £50 say – which is known in advance to both players. Figure 9.1 shows the decision tree for the game.

The method of backward induction tells us that, since player B must surely take the £50 at the final node, a rational player A should accept the pot of £49 at the penultimate node. Therefore player B should take the pot of money (£48) at the previous node and so on back to the initial node, where a rational player A should take the first £1 and end the game there and then. This is the sub-game perfect Nash equilibrium.

However, such reasoning is inconsistent with the assumption of common knowledge of rationality, where all players believe that all players are rational, and which dictates that such a game should end at the first node. It is redundant to ask what a player would do in the impossible event of a subsequent node being reached. These nodes should never be reached and so any argument based on this reasoning is spurious.

In reality, these games do not stop at the initial node; they go on for at least a few rounds. By behaving 'irrationally', the players do better than if they behaved selfishly and rationally. Some games have even been known to go right to the final node, with players splitting the £50 prize money, without having any prior agreement to do so (Dixit & Skeath, 1999). So it appears that, in games such as the centipede game and repeated martyrdom (prisoner's dilemma) games, where initial cooperation can make both players better off, a form of unspoken eudaemonic cooperation and a sense of fair play seems to usurp the rationality of backward induction, although how long such a spirit of cooperation would be maintained if the prize money at the first node was very large, is a moot point.

It is impossible to reconcile the flaws inherent in the concept of common knowledge of rationality since it attempts to impose a false certainty into a game where there is, by definition, uncertainty. In the centipede game, for example, it rules out the possibility of any player ever refusing the pot of money even though this is a legitimate choice (Romp, 1997). If player A does act irrationally and refuse the prize money, this provides incontrovertible evidence to player B that player A is not rational, and the progress of the game thereafter becomes uncertain. Player B might decide to string player A along for a while in the certain knowledge that the prize money will escalate and in the hope that player A will not suddenly turn rational and take the pot! And from player A's point of view, it becomes rational to pretend to be irrational, at least initially, in the hope that player B won't see through the ruse. Whatever the outcome or the procedure of the game, the assumption of common knowledge of rationality is demonstrably inconsistent.

Various attempts have been made to overcome the obstacles imposed by the need for some kind of rational consistency. Selten (1975) suggests that one way to resolve this inconsistency is to assume that players make random mistakes while playing games. This so-called *trembling hand assumption* allows a player in the centipede game to refuse the prize money without violating the assumption of rationality.

More radically, Binmore (1987) proposes redefining rationality as something *procedural*, requiring players to adopt arbitrary *stopping rules*. This model avoids situations where deviations from sub-game perfection are inconsistent with rationality, by defining different types of rationality simply in terms of alternative stopping rules.

Conclusion

Game theory clearly fails to describe the reality of decision making in some circumstances, although in its defense, it should be said that it primarily seeks to provide a prescriptive analysis that better equips players to make good strategic decisions. It does not make moral or ethical recommendations. It merely explores what happens when certain selfish incentives are assumed. Game theory cannot be held responsible for selfish behaviour, no more than medicine can be held responsible for sickness.

Game theory is in flux. It is continually being developed and researched. Not all predictions have been found to be supported by empirical evidence and this has led to refinement and reconstruction. So it should be! New and more complex variables have been introduced, largely as a result of its application to neo-classical and neo-Keynesian economics, though the extent to which in-game learning influences both success and rationality has not yet been fully explored. Fundamental questions such as whether learning increases pay-off or determines strategy, whether good learners play better games and which type of learning best equips players for which type of games, have been left unasked and unanswered. Such questions are of fundamental importance in education, training and organisational development, of course. The rapidly changing nature of society and its post-industrial economy brings new challenges almost daily. Information is no longer precious, the property of the privileged few. It is immediate, available in real time and irrespective of individual status. Organisational intelligence has thus become the shared faculty of the many, and the worth of collectives has become rooted in notions of social and intellectual capital.

If 'surviving and thriving in the face of change' is the name of the game, then everyone involved in it is a player. Individuals and organisations need to learn generic concepts of strategic networking and problem resolution, as a cultural expectation and over a lifetime. Decision making needs to be informed and sure-footed. The pay-off for keeping apace is effectiveness, the price for failing to do so is degeneration, and the strategy for avoiding failure lies at the interface of game theory and learning. It is an interaction that can only grow stronger.

A | Proof of the minimax theorem

Preamble

Suppose that the pay-off matrix for a two-person zero-sum game has m rows and n columns and that player 1 and player 2 choose their strategies, represented by row r_i and column c_j, simultaneously and with pay-off u_{ij}. Both players randomise their selections using mixed strategies in which a probability is assigned to each available option: p for player 1 and q for player 2 say). Of course, the sum of each player's mixed strategies is unity and can be written:

$$p = (p_1, p_2, \ldots, p_i, \ldots, p_m)$$

$\Sigma p_i = 1$, for $i = 1$ to m.

and

$$q = (q_1, q_2, \ldots, q_j, \ldots, q_n)$$

$\Sigma q_j = 1$, for $j = 1$ to n

Therefore, strategy r_i will be chosen with probability p_i and strategy c_j with probability q_j. These strategies are chosen independently, so the probability of getting a particular pay-off w_{ij} is $p_i q_j$. The expected pay-off for the game is then:

$\Sigma w_{ij} p_i q_j$, for $i = 1$ to m and $j = 1$ to n.

Player 1 wants to maximise this expected pay-off and player 2 to minimise it. If player 1 knew that player 2 was going to choose column c say, he or she would choose the strategy which maximised the expected pay-off:

$$\max_p \Sigma w_{ic} p_i q_c$$

Similarly, if player 2 knew that player 1 was going to choose row r say, he or she would choose the strategy which minimised the expected pay-off:

$$\min_q \Sigma w_{rj} p_r q_j$$

Although these counter-strategies cannot be used in practice since neither player knows what the other will do, the players can nevertheless maximise their security levels by assuming the most pessimistic choice by the opposing player. So player 1 can guarantee that the expected pay-off will not be less than:

$$\max_p \min_q \Sigma w_{ij} p_i q_j$$

and player 2 can guarantee that the expected pay-off will not be more than:

$$\min_q \max_p \Sigma w_{ij} p_i q_j$$

The minimax theorem states that these two expressions are equal. In other words:

$$\max_p \min_q \Sigma w_{ij} p_i q_j = \min_q \max_p \Sigma w_{ij} p_i q_j$$

for any pay-off matrix, denoted by (w_{ij}).

Proof: step 1

Since, by definition, the maximum value of a variable cannot be smaller than any other value and the minimum value cannot be bigger than any other value, it follows that

$$\max_p \min_q \Sigma w_{ij} p_i q_j = \min_q \Sigma w_{rj} p_r q_j \leq \Sigma w_{rc} p_r q_c \leq \max_p \Sigma w_{ic} p_i q_c$$
$$= \min_q \max_p \Sigma w_{ij} p_i q_j$$

So:

$$\boxed{\max_p \min_q \Sigma w_{ij} p_i q_j \leq \min_q \max_p \Sigma w_{ij} p_i q_j}$$

Teachers

	Strategy	Teach on	Passively supervise group study	Actively give revision workshops
Students	Attend lessons	20	8	13
	Do not attend lessons	0	10	9

Figure A.1

The intention is to now prove that:

$$\max_p \min_q \Sigma w_{ij} p_i q_j \geq \min_q \max_p \Sigma w_{ij} p_i q_j$$

thereby proving the theorem.

A graphic model for the game

If player 1 chooses row 1, say, and player 2 chooses a mixed strategy, then the expected pay-off will be:

$$w_{11}q_1 + w_{12}q_2 + \cdots + w_{1n}q_n = \Sigma w_{1j}q_j$$

If player 1 had chosen row 2 instead, then the expected pay-off would have been:

$$\Sigma w_{2j}q_j$$

and so on, for m possible rows. Therefore, any of player 2's mixed strategies can be represented graphically by a point in an m-dimension coordinate system, W, with m axes. That point can be written:

$$(\Sigma w_{1j}q_j, \Sigma w_{2j}q_j, \ldots, \Sigma w_{mj}q_j)$$

Consider the following example, in two dimensions, represented on Figure A.1. (This example can be contextualised by reference to Example 5.4.)

Every point in W corresponds to a strategy for player 2 and the vertices are the pure strategies (see Figures A.2 and A.3).

Any point inside W corresponds to a mixed strategy for player 2 corresponding to

(q_1, q_2, q_3), where $q_3 = 1 - (q_1 + q_2)$

	Player 2 chooses column 1	Player 2 chooses column 2	Player 2 chooses column 3
Player 1 chooses row 1	20	8	3
Player 1 chooses row 2	0	10	9
Vertex	(20, 0)	(8, 10)	(3, 9)

Figure A.2

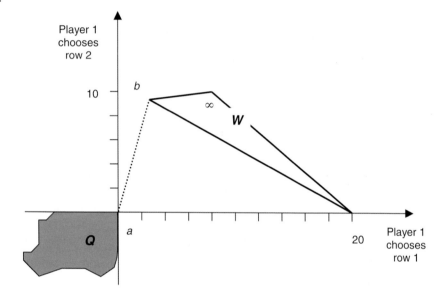

Figure A.3

For example, consider the point (8, 9). Clearly:

$$\Sigma w_{1j}q_j = 8 = 20q_1 + 8q_2 + 3(1 - q_1 - q_2)$$

and

$$\Sigma w_{2j}q_j = 9 = 0\,q_1 + 10q_2 + 9(1 - q_1 - q_2)$$

These two equations produce the following pair of simultaneous equations:

$$5 = 17q_1 + 5q_2$$

$$0 = q_2 - 9q_1$$

which in turn produce the following solution set:

$$q_1 = 5/62; \qquad q_2 = 45/62; \qquad q_3 = 12/62$$

So the point $(8, 9)$ corresponds to the mixed strategy $(5/62, 45/62, 12/62)$.

Proof: step 2

If

$$\min_q \max_p \Sigma w_{ij} p_i q_j > 0$$

then the coordinates of any point in W cannot *both* be negative. At least one must be zero or positive and therefore, the region of the third quadrant, Q, can have no common point with W.

Let $a = (a_1, a_2, \dots, a_m)$ be the point in Q nearest W, and $b = (b_1, b_2, \dots, b_m)$ be the point in W nearest a. Clearly, if a_i is replaced by a negative number a_i^* or zero, a is still a point in Q and is therefore no nearer W. In other words:

$$(b_1 - a_1{}^*)^2 + (b_2 - a_2)^2 + \cdots + (b_m - a_m)^2 \geq (b_1 - a_1)^2 \\ + (b_2 - a_2)^2 + \cdots + (b_m - a_m)^2$$

which simplifies after cancellation to:

$$(b_1 - a_1{}^*)^2 \geq (b_1 - a_1)^2$$

There are two cases to consider.

- If $b_1 \leq 0$, then possibly $a_1{}^* = b_1$, in which case $\boldsymbol{a_1} = \boldsymbol{b_1}$. Likewise $\forall$ a and b.
- If $b_1 > 0$ and if it is assumed that $a_1{}^* = 0$, then $b_1{}^2 \geq (b_1 - a_1)^2$, which simplifies to $(\boldsymbol{b_1} - \boldsymbol{a_1})$ $a_1 = 0$ because $a_1 \leq 0$ and $b_1 > 0$. Likewise $\forall$ a and b.

Proof: step 3

For any number t between 0 and 1 and any point $w \in W$, the point

$$tw + (1 - t)b = [tw_1 + (1 - t)b_1, tw_2 + (1 - t)b_2, \dots, \\ tw_m + (1 - t)b_m]$$

on the straight line between w and b is a probability weighted average of the points w and b. Since w and b are in W, they in turn are probability weighted averages of the vertices of W and therefore, so is the point $tw + (1 - t)b$.

So $t(w) + (1 - t)b$ also belongs to W and is thus no nearer to a than b. Thus:

$$[tw_1 + (1 - t)b_1 - a_1]^2 + [tw_2 + (1 - t)b_2 - a_2]^2 + \cdots$$
$$+ [tw_m + (1 - t)b_m - a_m]^2 \geq (b_1 - a_1)^2 + (b_2 - a_2)^2 + \cdots$$
$$+ (b_m - a_m)^2$$

If t is small, this expression becomes:

$$w_1(b_1 - a_1) + w_2(b_2 - a_2) + \cdots + w_m(b_m - a_m)$$
$$\geq (b_1 - a_1)^2 + (b_2 - a_2)^2 + \cdots + (b_m - a_m)^2$$

The right-hand side of this equation cannot be negative, therefore:

$$w_1(b_1 - a_1) + w_2(b_2 - a_2) + \cdots + w_m(b_m - a_m) \geq 0$$

Proof: step 4

Each of the numbers $(b_1 - a_1), (b_2 - a_2), \ldots, (b_m - a_m)$ is positive or zero, according to the result of step 2. They cannot all be zero, because a and b are different points and therefore cannot have *all* the same coordinates. Therefore, the sum of all these numbers is positive, i.e:

$$\Sigma(b_i - a_i) > 0$$

Therefore, if $(b_i - a_i)/\Sigma(b_i - a_i)$ is denoted by ξ_i, then $\xi_1, \xi_2, \ldots, \xi_m$ are each either zero or positive and $\Sigma\xi_i = 1$, since $\Sigma(b_i - a_i)/\Sigma(b_i - a_i) = 1$.

So $\xi = (\xi_1, \xi_2, \ldots, \xi_m)$ satisfies the requirements of a mixed strategy.

Dividing each term of the expression at the end of step 3 by $\Sigma(b_i - a_i)$ gives:

$$a_1\xi_1 + a_2\xi_2 + \cdots + a_m\xi_m > 0, \text{ for every } w \in W$$

But according to the definition of W in the graphic model, the coordinates of w are:

$$w = (\Sigma w_{1j}q_j, \Sigma w_{2j}q_j, \ldots, \Sigma w_{mj}q_j)$$

so a mixed strategy has therefore been found for player 1 such that:

$$\xi_1 \Sigma w_{1j} q_j + \xi_2 \Sigma w_{2j} q_j + \cdots + \xi_m \Sigma w_{mj} q_j > 0$$

for every q, so that:

$$\min_q \Sigma w_{ij} \xi_i q_j > 0$$

Since this holds for ξ, it must hold for the mixed-strategy p that maximises

$$\min_q \Sigma w_{ij} p_i q_j$$

Therefore:

$$\max_p \min_q \Sigma w_{ij} p_i q_j > 0$$

So it has been shown that:

> **if $\min_q \max_p \Sigma w_{ij} p_i q_j > 0$, then $\max_p \min_q \Sigma w_{ij} p_i q_j > 0$**

Proof: step 5

Let k be any number and consider the pay-off matrix which has $w_{ij} - k$ in place of w_{ij} everywhere. All pay-offs are reduced by k in both pure and mixed strategies. So:

$(\max_p \min_q \Sigma w_{ij} p_i q_j)$ is replaced by $(\max_p \min_q \Sigma w_{ij} p_i q_j - k)$

and

$(\min_q \max_p \Sigma w_{ij} p_i q_j)$ is replaced by $(\min_q \max_p \Sigma w_{ij} p_i q_j - k)$

It was proved in step 4 that:

if $(\min_q \max_p \Sigma w_{ij} p_i q_j - k) > 0$, then $(\max_p \min_q \Sigma w_{ij} p_i q_j - k) > 0$

So

if $\min_q \max_p \Sigma w_{ij} p_i q_j > k$, then $\max_p \min_q \Sigma w_{ij} p_i q_j > k$

Since k can be as close as necessary to $\min_q \max_p \Sigma w_{ij} p_i q_j$, it follows that:

$$\max_p \min_q \Sigma w_{ij} p_i q_j \geq \min_q \max_p \Sigma w_{ij} p_i q_j$$

But we have already seen that:

$$\max_p \min_q \Sigma w_{ij}p_iq_j \leq \min_q \max_p \Sigma w_{ij}p_iq_j$$

Therefore, the two must be equal, i.e:

$$\max_p \min_q \Sigma w_{ij}p_iq_j = \min_q \max_p \Sigma w_{ij}p_iq_j$$

B Proof of Bayes's theorem

Preamble

Bayes's theorem shows how a posteriori probabilities are calculated from a priori ones. In other words, how probabilities are updated as more information is received. In its simplest form it states:

$$p(A/B) = \frac{p(B/A)\ p(A)}{p(B/A)\ p(A) + p(B/A^c)\ p(A^c)}$$

where A^c denotes the complementary event of A such that:

$$p(A^c) = 1 - p(A)$$

and the a posteriori or *conditional* probability of event A happening, given that B has already happened, is denoted by $p(A/B)$.

Alternatively, if event B has a non-zero probability of occurring for each event A_i, of which there are n possibilities say, then Bayes's theorem may be stated as:

$$p(A_i/B) = \frac{p(B/A_i) \cdot p(A_i)}{\Sigma_i p(B/A_i) \cdot p(A_i)}$$

For example, if there are only two possibilities for A_i, then:

$$p(A_1/B) = \frac{p(B/A_1) \cdot p(A_1)}{p(B/A_1) \cdot p(A_1) + p(B/A_2) \cdot p(A_2)}$$

and

$$p(A_2/B) = \frac{p(B/A_2) \cdot p(A_2)}{p(B/A_1) \cdot p(A_1) + p(B/A_2) \cdot p(A_2)}$$

where $p(A_2) = 1 - p(A_1)$ of course.

Proof

By definition,

$$p(A_i \text{ and } B) = p(B/A_i) \cdot p(A_i)$$

and

$$p(A_i \text{ and } B) = p(A_i/B) \cdot p(B)$$

Equating these two gives:

$$p(A_i/B) = \frac{p(B/A_i) \cdot p(A_i)}{p(B)} \tag{1}$$

or

$$p(B) \cdot p(A_i/B) = p(B/A_i) \cdot p(A_i)$$

Summing both sides over i gives:

$$p(B) \, \Sigma_i p(A_i/B) = \Sigma_i p(B/A_i) \cdot p(A_i)$$

But we know that

$$\Sigma_i p(A_i/B) = 1$$

so

$$p(B) = \Sigma_i p(B/A_i) \cdot p(A_i) \tag{2}$$

Substituting (1) into (2) gives the result:

$$p(A_i/B) = \frac{p(B/A_i) \cdot p(A_i)}{\Sigma_i \; p(B/A_i) \cdot p(A_i)}$$

Bibliography

Abreu, D. (1986) Extremal equilibria of oligopolistic supergames, *Journal of Economic Theory*, Vol.39, No.1, pp.191–225.

Aliprantis, C. & Chakrabarti, S. (2000) *Games and Decision Making* (New York, Oxford University Press).

Aumann, R.J. (1975) Values of markets with a continuum of traders, *Econometrica*, Vol.43, No.4, pp.611–46.

Aumann, R.J. (1987) Correlated equilibrium as an expression of Bayesian ignorance, *Econometrica*, Vol.55, No.1, pp.1–18.

Aumann, R.J. (1988) *Preliminary Notes on Integrating Irrationality into Game Theory*, Mimeo, International Conference on Economic Theories of Politics, Haifa. [Quoted in McKelvey & Palfrey (1992)].

Aumann, R.J. (1989) Game theory, in: J. Eatwell, M. Milgate & P. Newman (Eds) *The New Palgrave: Game Theory* (London, Macmillan). [First published in 1987 as *The New Palgrave: A Dictionary of Economics.*]

Aumann, R.J. & Peleg, B. (1960) Von Neumann–Morgenstern solutions to cooperative games without side payments, *Bulletin of the American Mathematical Society*, Vol.66, pp.173–9.

Axelrod, R. (1981) The emergence of cooperation among egoists, *American Political Science Review*, Vol.75, No.2, pp.306–18.

Axelrod, R. (1984) *The Evolution of Cooperation* (New York, Basic Books). [1990 edition, London, Penguin Books.]

Bacon, N.T. (1897) *Researches into the Mathematical Principles of the Theory of Wealth by Augustin Cournot, 1838* (New York, Macmillan).

Banzhaf, J. (1965) Weighted voting doesn't work: a mathematical analysis, *Rutgers Law Review*, Vol.19, pp.317–43.

Beck, L.W. (1960) *A Commentary on Kant's Critique of Practical Reason* (Chicago, IL, University of Chicago Press).

Beck, L.W. (Ed) (1969) *Kant Studies Today* (La Salle, IL, Open Court).

Beck, L.W. (1988) *Kant Selections* (New York, Macmillan).

Benoit, J.P. & Krishna, V. (1985) Finitely repeated games, *Econometrica*, Vol.53, No.4, pp.905–22.

Benoit, J.P. & Krishna, V. (1987) Dynamic duopoly: prices and quantities, *Review of Economic Studies*, Vol.54, No.1(177), pp.23–35.

Bertrand, J. (1883) Theorie mathematique de la richesse sociale, par Leon Walras; recherches sur les principes mathematique de la theorie des richesses, par Augustin Cournot, *Journal des Savants*, September, pp.499–508.

Bierman, H.S. & Fernandez, L.F. (1998) *Game Theory with Economic Applications* (Reading, MA, Addison-Wesley). [2nd edition.]

Binmore, K. (1987) Modelling rational players (part I), *Economics and Philosophy*, Vol.3, No.2, pp.179–214.

Binmore, K.G. (1990) *Essays on the Foundation of Game Theory* (Oxford, Basil Blackwell).

Binmore, K. (1992) *Fun and Games: A Text on Game Theory* (Lexington, MA, D.C. Heath).

Borel, E. (1924) Sur les jeux ou intervennent l'hasard et l'habilite des joueurs, in: J. Hermann (Ed.) *Theorie des Probabilities*, pp.204–24 (Paris, Librairie Scientifique). Translation: Savage, L.J. (1953) On games that involve chance and the skill of players, *Econometrica*, Vol.21, No.1, pp.101–15.

Brams, S.J. (1990) *Negotiation Games: Applying Game Theory to Bargaining and Arbitration* (London, Routledge).

Bresnahan, T.F. (1981) Duopoly models with consistent conjectures, *American Economic Review*, Vol.71, No.5, pp.934–45.

Champsaur, P. (1975) Cooperation versus competition, *Journal of Economic Theory*, Vol.11, No.3, pp.394–417.

Colman, A.M. (1982) *Game Theory and Experimental Games: The Study of Strategic Interaction* (Oxford, Pergamon Press).

Corsi, J.R. (1981) Terrorism as a desperate game: fear, bargaining and communication in the terrorist event, *Journal of Conflict Resolution*, Vol.25, No.2, pp.47–85.

Cournot, A.A. (1838) *Recherches sur les Principes Mathematiques de la theorie des Richesses* (Paris). [See Bacon, N.T. for English edition.]

Cowen, R. & Fisher, P. (1998) Security council reform: a game theoretic analysis, *Mathematics Today*, Vol.34, No.4, pp.100–4.

David, F.N. (1962) *Games, Gods and Gambling: The Origins and History of Probability and Statistical Ideas from the Earliest Times to the Newtonian Era* (London, Charles Griffin).

Deegan, J. & Packel, E.W. (1978) A new index of power for simple *n*-person games, *International Journal of Game Theory*, Vol.7, Issue 2, pp.113–23.

Dimand, R.W. & Dimand, M.A. (1992) The early history of the theory of strategic games from Waldegrave to Borel, in: E.R. Weintraub (Ed.) *Toward a History of Game Theory* (Durham, NC, Duke University Press).

Dixit, A.K. & Nalebuff, B.J. (1991) *Thinking Strategically: The Competitive Edge in Business, Politics, and Everyday Life* (New York, Norton).

Dixit, A. & Skeath, S. (1999) *Games of Strategy* (New York, Norton).

Eatwell, J., Milgate, M. & Newman, P. (Eds) (1989) *The New Palgrave: Game Theory* (London, Macmillan). [First published in 1987 as *The New Palgrave: A Dictionary of Economics*.]

Edgeworth, F.Y. (1881) *Mathematical Psychics: an Essay on the Applications of Mathematics to the Moral Sciences* (London, Kegan Paul). [Reprinted, 1967, New York, Augustus M. Kelley.]

Farquharson, R. (1969) *Theory of Voting* (Oxford, Basil Blackwell).

Frechet, M. (1953) Emile Borel, initiator of the theory of psychological games and its application, *Econometrica*, Vol.21, No.1, pp.118–24. [Followed immediately by: J. von Neumann, *Communication on the Borel Notes*, pp.124–7].

Friedman, J.W. (1986) *Game Theory with Applications to Economics* (Oxford, Oxford University Press). [1990 edition.]

Friedman, M. (1953) *Essays in Positive Economics* (Chicago, IL, University of Chicago Press).

Gale, D. & Shapley, L.S. (1962) College admissions and the stability of marriage, *American Mathematical Monthly*, Vol.69, pp.9–15.

Gamson, W.A. (1961) A theory of coalition formation, *American Sociological Review*, Vol.26, No.3, pp.373–82.

Gibbons, R. (1992a) *A Primer in Game Theory* (London, Prentice Hall).

Gibbons, R. (1992b) *Game Theory for Applied Economists* (Princeton, NJ, Princeton University Press).

Gillies, D.B. (1959) Solutions to general non-zero-sum games, in: A.W. Tucker & R.D. Luce (Eds) *Contributions to the Theory of Games Vol.IV, Annals of Mathematics Studies Number 40*, pp.47–85 (Princeton, NJ, Princeton University Press).

Guyer, P. & Wood, A.W. (1998) *Immanuel Kant: Critique of Pure Reason* (Cambridge, Cambridge University Press).

Gordon, R.J. (1990) What is new-Keynesian economics? *Journal of Economic Literature*, Vol.28, No.3, pp.1115–71.

Hagenmayer, S.J. (1995) Albert W. Tucker, 89, Famed Mathematician, *Philadelphia Inquiries*, Thursday, February 2, p.B7

Hargreaves Heap, S.P. & Varoufakis, Y. (1995) *Game Theory: A Critical Introduction* (London, Routledge).

Harris, R.J. (1969) Note on Howard's theory of meta-games, *Psychological Reports*, Vol.24, pp.849–50.

Harsanyi, J.C. (1966) A general theory of rational behaviour in game situations, *Econometrica*, Vol.34, No.3, pp.613–34.

Harsanyi, J.C. (1967) Games with incomplete information played by 'Bayesian' players, I–III, *Management Science*, Part I in:Vol.14, No.3, pp.159–82. Part II in: Vol.14, No.5, pp.320–34. Part III in: Vol.14, No.7, pp.486–503.

Harsanyi, J.C. & Selten, R. (1972) A generalised Nash solution for two-person bargaining games with incomplete information, *Management Science*, Vol.18, No.5, Part 2, pp.80–106.

Hart, S. (1977) Asymptotic value of games with a continuum of players, *Journal of Mathematical Economics*, Vol.4, pp.57–80.

Hey, J.D. (1991) *Experiments in Economics* (Oxford, Blackwell).

Howard, N. (1966) The theory of metagames, *General Systems*, Vol.11, Part V, pp.167–86.

Jenkinson, T. (Ed.) (2000) *Readings in Microeconomics* (Oxford, Oxford University Press). [Papers originally published in the first fourteen volumes of the *Oxford Review of Economic Policy*.]

Johnston, R.J. (1978) On the measurement of power: some reactions to Laver, *Environment and Planning A*, Vol.10, No.8, pp.907–14.

Kagel, J.H. & Roth, A.E. (1995) *The Handbook of Experimental Economics* (Princeton, NJ, Princeton University Press).

Kelley, H.H., Thibaut, J.W., Radloff, R. & Mundy, D. (1962) The development of cooperation in the 'minimal social situation', *Psychological Monographs*, Vol.76, No.19, Whole No. 538.

Kuhn, H.W. (1953) Extensive games and the problem of information, in: H.W. Kuhn & A. Tucker (Eds) *Contributions to the Theory of Games Vol.II, Annals of Mathematics Studies Number 28*, pp.193–216 (Princeton, NJ, Princeton University Press).

Kreps, D.M. (1990) *Game Theory and Economic Modelling* (Oxford, Clarendon Press).

Kreps, D.M., Milgrom, P., Roberts, J. & Wilson, R. (1982) Rational cooperation in the finitely repeated prisoner's dilemma, *Journal of Economic Theory*, Vol.27, No.2, pp.245–52.

Leonard, R.J. (1992), Creating a context for game theory, in: E.R. Weintraub (Ed.) *Toward a History of Game Theory* (Durham, NC, Duke University Press).

Lewis, D.K. (1969) *Convention: a Philosophical Study* (Cambridge, MA, Harvard University Press).

Luce, R.D. & Raiffa, H. (1989) *Games and Decisions: Introduction and Critical Survey* (New York, Dover). [Originally published, 1957, New York, Wiley.]

Lyons, B. & Varoufakis, Y. (1989) Game theory, oligopoly and bargaining, in: J.D. Hey (Ed.) *Current Issues in Microeconomics* (Basingstoke, Macmillan).

Mann, I. & Shapley, L.S. (1964) The a priori voting strength of the electoral college, in: M. Shubik (Ed.) *Game Theory and Related Approaches to Social Behaviour*, pp.151–64 (New York, Wiley).

Mas-Colell, A. (1977) Competitive and value allocations of large exchange economies, *Journal of Economic Theory*, Vol.14, No.2, pp.419–38.

Maynard Smith, J. (1982) *Evolution and the Theory of Games* (Cambridge, Cambridge University Press).

McKelvey, R.D. & Niemi, R.G. (1978) A multistage game representation of sophisticated voting for binary procedures, *Journal of Economic Theory*, Vol.18, No.1, pp.1–22.

McKelvey, R.D. & Palfrey, T.R. (1992) An experimental study of the centipede game, *Econometrica,* Vol.60, No.4, pp.803–36.

Megiddo, N. (1986) *Remarks on Bounded Rationality*, Technical Report, IBM Research Report, RJ 54310, Computer Science. [Quoted in McKelvey & Palfrey (1992).]

Milnor, J. & Shapley, L.S. (1957) On games of survival, in: M. Dresher, A.W. Tucker & P. Wolfe (Eds) *Contributions to the Theory of Games Vol.III, Annals of Mathematics Studies Number 39*, pp.15–45 (Princeton, NJ, Princeton University Press).

Mirowski, P. (1991) When games grow deadly serious: the military influence on the evolution of game theory, in: C.D. Goodwin (Ed.) *Economics and National Security* (Durham, NC, Duke University Press).

Mitchell, C.R. & Banks, M. (1996) *Handbook of Conflict Resolution: the Analytical Problem-Solving Approach* (London, Pinter).

Morgenstern, O. (1976) The collaboration between Oskar Morgenstern and John von Neumann on the theory of games, *Journal of Economic Literature*, Vol.14, No.3, pp.805–16.

Myerson, R.B. (1984) Cooperative games with incomplete information, *International Journal of Game Theory*, Vol.13, No.2, pp.69–96.

Nasar, S. (1998) *A Beautiful Mind: The Life of Mathematical Genius and Nobel Laureate John Nash* (London, Faber).

Nash, J.F. (1950) Equilibrium points in n-person games, *Proceedings of the National cademy of Sciences of the United States of America*, Vol.36, No.1, pp.48–9.

Nash, J. (1951) Non co-operative games, *Annals of Mathematics*, Vol.54, No.2, pp.286–95.

O'Neill, B. (1987) Nonmetric test of the minimax theory of two-person zerosum games, *Proceedings of the National Academy of Sciences of the United States of America*, Vol.84, No.7, pp.2106–9.

Peleg, B. (1963) Solutions to cooperative games without side payments, *Transactions of the American Mathematical Society*, Vol.106, pp.280–92.

Phlips, L. (1995) *Competition policy: a Game Theoretic Perspective* (Cambridge, Cambridge University Press).

Plon, M. (1974) On the meaning of the notion of conflict and its study in social psychology, *European Journal of Social Psychology*, Vol.4, pp.389–436.

Poundstone, W. (1993) *Prisoner's Dilemma: John von Neumann, Game Theory, and the Puzzle of the Bomb* (Oxford, Oxford University Press). [First published, 1922, New York, Doubleday.]

Radner, R. (1980) Collusive behaviour in noncooperative epsilon-equilibria of oligopolies with long but finite lives, *Journal of Economic Theory*, Vol.22, No.2, pp.136–56.

Rapoport, A. (1967a) Exploiter, leader, hero and martyr: the four archetypes of the 2×2 game, *Behavioral Science*, Vol.12, pp.81–4.

Rapoport, A. (1967b) Escape from paradox, *Scientific American*, Vol.217, No.1, pp.50–6.

Rapoport, A (1989) Prisoner's dilemma, in: J. Eatwell, M. Milgate & P. Newman (Eds) *The New Palgrave: Game Theory* (London, Macmillan). [Originally published as *The New Palgrave: A Dictionary of Economics*, 1987.]

Rapoport, A. & Guyer, M. (1966) A taxonomy of 2×2 games, *General Systems*, Vol.11, Part V, pp.203–14.

Rapoport, A. & Orwant, C. (1962) Experimental games: a review, *Behavioral Science*, Vol.7, pp.1–37.

Rees, R. (1993) Tacit collusion, *Oxford Review of Economic Policy*, Vol.9, No.2, pp.27–40.

Riker, W.H. (1962) *The Theory of Political Coalitions* (New Haven, CT, Yale University Press).

Riker, W.H. (1992) The entry of game theory into political science, in: E.R. Weintraub (Ed.) *Toward a History of Game Theory* (Durham, NC, Duke University Press).

Riker, W.H. & Ordeshook, P.C. (1973) *An Introduction to Positive Political Theory* (Englewood Cliffs, NJ, Prentice Hall).

Robinson, M. (1975) Prisoner's dilemma: metagames and other solutions (critique and comment), *Behavioral Science*, Vol.20, pp.201–5.

Romp, G. (1997) *Game Theory: Introduction and Applications* (Oxford, Oxford University Press).

Rosenthal, R.W. (1979) Sequence of games with varying opponents, *Econometrica*, Vol.47, No.6, pp.1353–66.

Rosenthal, R.W. (1980) New equilibria for non-cooperative two-person games, *Journal of Mathematical Sociology*, Vol.7, No.1, pp.15–26.

Rosenthal, R.W. (1981) Games of perfect information, predatory pricing, and the chain-store paradox, *Journal of Economic Theory*, Vol.25, No.1, pp.92–100.

Rosenthal, R.W. & Landau, H.J. (1979) A game-theoretic analysis of bargaining with reputations, *Journal of Mathematical Psychology*, Vol.20, No.3, pp.233–55.

Rosenthal, R.W. & Rubinstein, A. (1984) Repeated two-player games with ruin, *International Journal of Game Theory*, Vol.13, No.3, pp.155–77.

Sauage, L.J. (1954) *The Foundation of Statistics* (New York, John Wiley).

Scarf, H.E. (1967) The core of an *n* person game, *Econometrica*, Vol.35, No.1, pp.50–69.

Schelling, T.C. (1960) *The Strategy of Conflict* (Cambridge, MA, Harvard University Press). [1980 edition.]

Schmalensee, R. & Willig, R.D. (Eds) (1989) *Handbook of Industrial Organisation* (Amsterdam, Elsevier Science/North-Holland). [2 vols.]

Selten, R. (1975) The reexamination of the perfectness concept for equilibrium points in extensive games, *International Journal of Game Theory*, Vol.4, Issue 1, pp.25–55.

Selten, R. (1978) The chain-store paradox, *Theory and Decision*, Vol.9, No.2, pp.127–59.

Selten, R. (1980) A note on evolutionary stable strategies in asymmetric animal conflicts, *Journal of Theoretical Biology*, Vol.84, No.1, pp.93–101.

Shapley, L.S. (1953) A value for *n*-person games, in: H.W. Kuhn & A.W. Tucker (Eds) *Contributions to the Theory of Games Vol.II, Annals of Mathematics Studies Number 28*, pp.307–18 (Princeton, NJ, Princeton University Press).

Shapley, L.S. & Shubik, M. (1954) A method for evaluating the distribution of power in a committee system, *American Political Science Review*, Vol.48, No.3, pp.787–92.

Shapley, L.S. & Shubik, M. (1969) Pure competition, coalitional power and fair division, *International Economic Review*, Vol.10, No.3, pp.337–62.

Shapley, L.S. & Snow, R.N. (1950) Basic solutions of discrete games, in: H.W. Kuhn & A.W. Tucker (Eds) *Contributions to the Theory of Games Vol.I, Annals of Mathematics Studies Number 24*, pp.27–35 (Princeton, NJ, Princeton University Press).

Shubik, M. (1959) Edgeworth market games, in: A.W. Tucker & R.D. Luce (Eds) *Contributions to the Theory of Games Vol.IV, Annals of Mathematical Studies Number 40*, pp.267–78 (Princeton, N.J., Princeton University Press).

Sidowski, J.B. (1957) Reward and punishment in a minimal social situation, *Journal of Experimental Psychology*, Vol.54, No.5, pp.318–26.

Simon, H.A. (1997) *Models of Bounded Rationality, Vol.3: Empirically Grounded Economic Reason* (Cambridge, MA., MIT Press).

Straffin, P.D. (1977) Homogeneity, independence, and power indices, *Public Choice*, Vol.30, pp.107–18. [Quoted in: Riker, W.H. (1992) The entry of game theory into political science, in: E.R. Weintraub (Ed.) *Toward a History of Game Theory* (Durham, NC, Duke University Press).]

Sugden, R. (1991) Rational choice: a survey of contributions from economics and philosophy, *Economic Journal*, July, Vol.101, pp.751–85.

Todhunter, I. (1865) *A History of the Mathematical Theory of Probability* (Cambridge, Cambridge University Press). [Reprinted 1965.]

Touraine, A. (1969) *La Société Post-Industrielle (Paris, Editions Denoel). Translation: Mayhew, L.F.X. (1974) The Post-Industrial Society* (London, Wildwood House).

Ville, J.A. (1938) Sur la theorie generale des jeux ou intervient l'habilite des joueurs, in: Borel, E. (Ed.) *Traite du Calcul des Probabilites et de ses Applications*, Vol.4, pp.105–13 (Paris, Gauthier-Villars).

Von Neumann, J. (1928) Zur Theorie der Gesellschaftsspiele, *Mathematische Annalen*, Band 100, pp.295–320. Translation: Bargmann, S. (1959) On the theory of games and strategy, in: R.D. Luce & A.W. Tucker (Eds) *Contributions to the Theory of Games Vol.IV, Annals of Mathematics Studies Number 40*, pp.13–42 (Princeton, NJ, Princeton University Press).

Von Neumann, J. (1937) Uber ein Okonomisches Gleichungssystem und eine Verallgemeinerung des Brouwerschen Fixpunktsatzes, in: Menger, K. *Ergebnisse eines Mathematischen Seminars* (Vienna). Translation: Morgenstern, G. (1945) A model of general economic equilibrium, *Review of Economic Studies*, Vol.13, No.1, pp.1–9.

Von Neumann, J. & Morgenstern, O. (1953) *Theory of Games and Economic Behaviour* (Princeton, NJ, Princeton University Press). [First published in 1944.]

Von Stackelberg, H. (1934) *Marktform und Gleichgewicht* (Vienna, Springer). [As described in: H. Von Stackelberg (1952) *The Theory of the Market Economy* (London, Hodge). Translation: Peacock, A.T. (First published in 1943 as *Grundlagen der Theoretischen Volkswirtschaftslehre*).]

Wald, A. (1945) Statistical decision functions which minimise maximum risk, *Annals of Mathematics*, Vol.46, No.2, pp.265–80.

Weyl, H. (1950) Elementary proof of a minimax theorem due to von Neumann, in: H.W. Kuhn & A.W. Tucker (Eds) *Contributions to the Theory of Games Vol.I, Annals of Mathematics Studies Number 24*, pp. 19–25 (Princeton, NJ, Princeton University Press).

Wilson, R. (1978) Information, efficiency, and the core of an economy, *Econometrica*, Vol.46, No.4, pp.807–16.

Zermelo, E. (1913) Uber eine Anwendung der Mengenlehre auf die Theorie des Schachspiels, in: E.W.Hobson & A.E.H. Love (Eds) *Proceedings of the Fifth International Congress of Mathematicians, Cambridge, 22–28 August, 1912*, Vol.2, pp.501–4 (Cambridge, Cambridge University Press).

Index